Verbal Behavior Targets
A Tool to Teach Mands, Tacts and Intraverbals

Diana Luckevich, Ph.D.

Verbal Behavior Targets
A Tool to Teach Mands, Tacts and Intraverbals

Copyright © 2008 Diana Luckevich

Published by: Different Roads to Learning
                  121 West 27th Street
                  New York, NY 10001

                  Telephone: 1-800-853-1057
                  Fax: 1-212-604-9637

ISBN 978-0-9755859-4-8
Library of Congress Control Number: 2008934624

Book Layout: Diana Luckevich
Cover Art: Fresh Concentrate

Printed in the United States of America

Table of Contents

Chapter 5 – Category, Feature and Function

Chapter 6 – Conversation Topics

Introduction

Verbal Behavior Targets, A Tool to Teach Mands, Tacts and Intraverbals is an instructional resource for teaching young children with autism, PDD, Down syndrome or other language delays. This book supports the implementation of a verbal behavior program or similar language instruction. It contains targets aimed at teaching language to children who have skills in the range of non-verbal to pre-conversational. This book provides lists of common and practical language to teach a child. Therapists, clinicians, teachers, and parents can use this book to help children improve their communication.

The verbal behavior targets provided in this book support the communication needs of early language learners. The targets include words, phrases, sentences and questions that are grouped into categories. Targets should be selected to meet the unique language goals of each individual child. This book is not a curriculum that explains the sequence of language development and guides one in making decisions about what to teach and when to teach it. Instead, it is a resource that provides targets to meet the goals outlined in a language curriculum.

Verbal behavior programs focus on teaching language skills following concepts described in B.F. Skinner's book Verbal Behavior. Skinner (1957) describes language as behavior of a speaker accompanied by a listener. He defines verbal operants that support communication behaviors. Three of these verbal operants are the mand, the tact and the intraverbal. A mand is a command or request for an object or action from a listener. A tact is a verbal response produced in the presence of an object or action. A tact is expressed as a verbal label of an object seen by the speaker. The intraverbal is a response to another speaker's language. Intraverbals include answers to questions, comments and other language that is invoked from listening to another person.

Chapter 1
Words

The targets in each category are listed in alphabetical order to help you record student progress data. However, you should consider teaching targets to a child out of alphabetical order because it is easier for children to learn multiple words at the same time when the words start with different first letters and have a variable number of syllables. Words that sound different are easier to discriminate and learn.

This book can be used to record a student's progress with these language targets. There are data sheets at the end of the book and space to write in additional targets in many of the categories. A **Notes** area is provided to the right of each target to record a student's milestones with that target. A list of language milestones that might be measured is provided below.

Language Milestones

Receptive

Expressive

Signs

Echoic

Mand

Tact

Intraverbal

Says with an peer

Generalized with new material

Spontaneous

Read

In the **Notes** area, depending on the data collection methodology, one may choose to record the start date, mastered date, or reviewed date of a milestone for a target. For example a notation like R - 4/12, 5/03 E - 5/04, 5/11 may represent that for a single target the receptive training began on 4/12 and was considered mastered on 5/03, then expressive training began on 5/04 and was mastered on 5/11.

4

Verbal Behavior Targets - A Tool to Teach Mands, Tacts and Intraverbals

Animal

Animal	Notes	Animal	Notes
aardvark		orangutang	
anteater		otter	
ape		ox	
bat		panda	
bear		pig	
beaver		polar bear	
bull		pony	
bunny		puppy	
calf		rabbit	
camel		raccoon	
cat		rat	
cheetah		reindeer	
chimpanzee		rhinoceros	
cow		sheep	
deer		skunk	
dinosaur		snake	
dog		squirrel	
donkey		stallion	
elephant		tiger	
elk		warthog	
fox		weasel	
gerbil		wolf	
giraffe		woodchuck	
goat		yak	
goose		zebra	
gorilla			
guinea pig			
hamster			
horse			
hyena			
jaguar			
kangaroo			
kitten			
koala			
llama			
lamb			
lion			
lizard			
monkey			
moose			
mouse			

Animal

Animal Part	Notes		Bird	Notes
antenna			bird	
antler			blue jay	
beak			chick	
claw			chicken	
fang			crow	
feather			dove	
fin			duck	
fur			duckling	
gill			eagle	
hoof			flamingo	
horn			goose	
mane			hen	
paw			heron	
scale			hummingbird	
shell			mockingbird	
spot			ostrich	
stripe			owl	
tail			parakeet	
tentacle			parrot	
tusk			peacock	
whisker			pelican	
wing			penguin	
			pigeon	
			quail	
			robin	
			rooster	
			seagull	
			sparrow	
			swan	
			toucan	
			turkey	
			vulture	
			woodpecker	

Animal

Animal - Insect	Notes		Notes
ant			
bee			
beetle			
bug			
butterfly			
caterpillar			
centipede			
cockroach			
crane fly			
cricket			
dragonfly			
earthworm			
firefly			
flea			
fly			
fruit fly			
gnat			
grasshopper			
hornet			
lady bug			
lice			
maggot			
mite			
mosquito			
moth			
praying mantis			
slug			
spider			
tarantula			
termites			
tick			
wasp			
worm			

Animal

Sea Life	Notes	Animal-Water	Notes
barracuda		alligator	
clown fish		crocodile	
crab		duck	
dolphin		fish	
eel		flounder	
jellyfish		frog	
lobster		goldfish	
octopus		guppy	
otter		hippo	
sea horse		platypus	
seal		salmon	
shark		snail	
shrimp		toad	
star fish		turtle	
sting ray		walrus	
tropical fish			
tuna fish			
whale			
sea otter			

Clothing

Accessory	Notes	Clothes	Notes
back pack		bathing suit	
barrette		bikini	
belt		coat	
bib		diaper	
bow		dress	
bracelet		hoodie	
brief case		jacket	
buckle		jeans	
button		nightgown	
computer case		overalls	
earring		pajamas	
fanny pack		pants	
glasses		parka	
gloves		raincoat	
goggles		shirt	
hand bag		shorts	
hood		skirt	
jewelry		snowsuit	
mitten		sweat pants	
necklace		sweater	
pocket		sweatshirt	
purse		swim trunks	
ribbon		swimsuit	
ring		tank top	
scarf		t-shirt	
sleeve		underpants	
snap		undershirt	
sunglasses		underwear	
tie		vest	
Velcro			
wallet			
watch			
zipper			

Clothing

Footwear	Notes	Headwear	Notes
boots		bandana	
cleats		baseball cap	
flip flops		cap	
flippers		cowboy hat	
rain boots		ear muffs	
sandals		hat	
shoes		headband	
slippers		helmet	
sneakers		shower cap	
snow boots		visor	
socks			

Event

Birthday Party	Notes
balloon	
banner	
birthday cake	
birthday hat	
bow	
candles	
card	
confetti	
cups	
decorations	
envelope	
favors	
flame	
forks	
friends	
games	
gift	
ice cream	
invitation	
make a wish	
napkins	
noise maker	
paper plates	
pin the tail on the donkey	
piñata	
plates	
present	
ribbon	
table cloth	
thank you card	
wrapping paper	

Daily Living	Notes
appointment	
bath time	
bed time	
bike ride	
breakfast	
dentist visit	
dinner	
doctor visit	
eye exam	
lunch	
meeting	
nap	
play	
playground	
recess	
restaurant	
show	
shower	
story time	
visit	

Event

Holiday	Notes		Special	Notes
April Fools Day			amusement park	
Christmas			barbeque	
Cinco De Mayo			birthday	
Columbus Day			carnival	
Easter			concert	
Election Day			fair	
Father's Day			miniature golf	
Flag Day			movie	
Fourth of July			museum	
Good Friday			parade	
Ground Hog Day			party	
Halloween			presentation	
Hanukkah			rodeo	
Independence Day			roller rink	
Kwanzaa			skating rink	
Labor Day			theatre	
Martin Luther King's Day				
Memorial Day				
Mother's Day				
New Year's Day				
New Year's Eve				
Passover				
President's Day				
Ramadan				
Rosh Hashanah				
St Patrick's Day				
Thanksgiving				
Valentine's Day				
Veteran's Day				

Food

Breakfast	Notes	Lunch	Notes
apple juice		bread	
bacon		bun	
bagel		carrot sticks	
butter		cheese	
cereal		chicken nuggets	
cereal bar		chicken salad	
cream cheese		coleslaw	
cream of rice		cottage cheese	
cream of wheat		French fries	
eggs		fruit	
English muffin		grilled cheese	
French toast		ham	
fried egg		hamburger	
fruit		hot dog	
granola bar		jelly	
honey		mayonnaise	
milk		peanut butter	
muffin		potato salad	
oatmeal		salad	
omelet		sandwich	
orange juice		soup	
pancakes		tuna fish	
sausage		turkey	
scrambled eggs			
syrup			
toast			
waffles			
yogurt			

Food

Dinner	Notes	Dessert	Notes
baked potato		brownie	
bread		cake	
breadsticks		candy	
chicken		chocolate	
chicken rolls		chocolate chip cookie	
crust		chocolate syrup	
French fries		cookies	
fried chicken		Danish	
hamburger		donut	
hotdog		fruit	
ketchup		gingerbread	
lamb chops		hot fudge	
macaroni and cheese		ice cream	
mashed potatoes		marshmallow	
meat		oatmeal cookie	
noodles		peanut butter cookie	
onion rings		pie	
pizza		sundae	
ribs		whipped cream	
rice			
roast beef			
salad			
soup			
spaghetti			
steak			
stew			
tomato sauce			
vegetables			

Food

Drink	Notes		Fruit	Notes
apple cider			apple	
apple juice			applesauce	
cocoa			banana	
coffee			blackberry	
hot chocolate			blueberry	
ice			cantaloupe	
iced coffee			cherry	
iced tea			grapefruit	
juice			grapes	
Kool-aid			honeydew	
lemonade			kiwi	
milk			lemon	
orange juice			lime	
pop			mango	
soda			nectarine	
tea			olive	
water			orange	
			peach	
			pear	
			pineapple	
			plum	
			prunes	
			raisin	
			raspberry	
			strawberry	
			watermelon	

Food

Meat	Notes		Snack	Notes
bacon			chips	
bologna			cookie	
burger			cracker	
chicken			fruit rollup	
corndog			gummy bears	
corned beef			jelly beans	
fish			nuts	
ham			peanuts	
hamburger			popcorn	
hot dog			pretzels	
lamb chops			rice cake	
pastrami				
pork chops				
ribs				
roast beef				
salami				
sausage				
steak				
turkey				

Verbal Behavior Targets - A Tool to Teach Mands, Tacts and Intraverbals

Food

Vegetable	Notes	Ingredient	Notes
asparagus		baking powder	
beans		baking soda	
beets		brown sugar	
broccoli		eggs	
brussel sprouts		flour	
cabbage		garlic	
carrot		honey	
cauliflower		ketchup	
celery		margarine	
corn		mayonnaise	
cucumber		molasses	
eggplant		mustard	
green bean		oil	
green pepper		pepper	
lettuce		salt	
mushroom		spices	
onion		sugar	
peas		vanilla	
pepper		vinegar	
pickle			
potato			
pumpkin			
radish			
red pepper			
spinich			
squash			
sweet potato			
tomato			
yellow squash			
zucchini			

Health

Body Part	Notes		Body Part	Notes
ankle			mustache	
arm			neck	
armpit			nose	
back			palm	
beard			pinky finger	
belly			pointer finger	
belly button			ring finger	
body			shin	
bottom			shoulder	
brain			skeleton	
butt			smile	
calf			stomach	
cheek			sweat	
chest			teeth	
chin			thigh	
ear			throat	
elbow			thumb	
eyebrow			toes	
eyelash			tongue	
eyelid			tooth	
eyes			tummy	
face			waist	
feet			wrist	
fingernail				
fingers				
fist				
foot				
forehead				
gums				
hair				
hands				
head				
heart				
heel				
knee				
knuckle				
leg				
lips				
missing tooth				
mouth				
muscle				

Health

Exercise	Notes
bike ride	
jog	
jump rope	
jumping jacks	
push up	
run	
sit up	
skip	
stair step	
stretch	
swim	
walk	
yoga	

Health	Notes
better	
careful	
fit	
good	
heal	
healthy	
safe	
well	

Health

Sick	Notes		Notes
aspirin			
band aid			
bandage			
boo boo			
bruise			
bump			
catch			
check up			
cold			
cough			
cough syrup			
dropper			
flu			
hurt			
ill			
medicine			
pain			
painful			
shot			
thermometer			
treat			
vomit			
x-ray			

House - Bathroom

Item	Notes	Furniture	Notes
brush		bathtub	
bubble bath		counter	
clippers		faucet	
comb		hamper	
conditioner		makeup mirror	
cotton balls		medicine cabinet	
dental floss		mirror	
deodorant		nozzle	
gel		potty	
hair spray		shower	
hairdryer		shower door	
lipstick		shower filter	
loofah		shower head	
lotion		shower massager	
makeup		sink	
medicine		tissue holder	
perfume		toilet	
powder		towel bar	
Q-tips		urinal	
scale		vanity	
shampoo		whirlpool	
shaver			
shaving cream			
shower curtain			
shower gel			
soap			
spray			
tissue			
toilet paper			
toothpaste			
toothbrush			
towel			
tweezers			
vitamins			
wash cloth			

House - Bedroom

Item	Notes		Furniture	Notes
bedspread			bed	
blanket			bookcase	
comforter			box spring	
cover			bunk bed	
curtains			changing table	
hanger			closet	
light			crib	
night light			drawer	
pillow			dresser	
pillowcase			frame	
quilt			mattress	
sheets			nightstand	
toys			window	

House - Kitchen

Item	Notes	Item	Notes
aluminum foil		rolling pin	
baking dish		scraper	
bowl		scrubber	
cabinet		sharp knife	
cake pan		silverware	
candle		sponge	
container		spoon	
cookie sheet		stove	
counter		strainer	
cup		straw	
cupboard		tablecloth	
dishes		teapot	
drawer		timer	
foil		tin foil	
fork		tongs	
frying pan		toothpick	
glass		vase	
grater		vegetable peeler	
groceries		water filter	
high chair		wax paper	
kettle			
knife			
ladle			
measuring cup			
measuring spoon			
muffin tin			
mug			
napkin			
pan			
paper towel			
peeler			
pie pan			
pitcher			
placemat			
plastic bag			
plastic wrap			
plate			
plug			
pot			
rag			

Verbal Behavior Targets - A Tool to Teach Mands, Tacts and Intraverbals

House - Kitchen

Appliance	Notes		Notes
blender			
bread machine			
can opener			
crock pot			
deep fryer			
dishwasher			
dryer			
electric fry pan			
food processor			
freezer			
grill			
juicer			
microwave			
mixer			
oven			
popcorn popper			
range			
refrigerator			
rice cooker			
stove			
toaster			
toaster oven			
waffle iron			
washer			

House – Living room

Item	Notes
books	
fan	
fire place tools	
frame	
lamp	
lamp shade	
mantle	
newspaper	
remote control	
rug	
seat	
shelf	
TV	
vase	
wood	

Furniture	Notes
air conditioner	
bookshelf	
chair	
coffee table	
couch	
desk	
end table	
entertainment center	
fire place	
foot stool	
love seat	
playpen	
recliner	
rocking chair	
sofa	
sofa table	
table	
TV stand	

House - Room

Room Part	Notes	Room	Notes
blinds		basement	
carpet		bathroom	
ceiling		bedroom	
corner		den	
curtains		dining room	
door		family room	
door handle		foyer	
door knob		garage	
floor		hall way	
light switch		kitchen	
shades		laundry room	
smoke detector		living room	
wall		office	
window		pantry	
		playroom	

Household

Electronic	Notes		Things	Notes
alarm clock			bag	
calculator			basket	
camera			batteries	
CD player			bottle	
clock			box	
computer			clothes pin	
disk			detergent	
DVD player			dish liquid	
fan			door knob	
headphones			garbage can	
IPod			ironing board	
iron			jar	
microphone			key	
mouse			leash	
MP3			lid	
Playstation			light bulb	
printer			lunch bag	
radio			lunch box	
sewing machine			measuring tape	
stereo			newspaper	
video camera			paper bag	
video games			phone book	
Wii			photo	
X Box			picture	
			push pin	
			smoke detector	
			telephone	
			telephone book	
			ticket	
			trash can	
			tray	
			walkie talkie	
			waste basket	

Verbal Behavior Targets - A Tool to Teach Mands, Tacts and Intraverbals

Other Items

Instrument	Notes		Material	Notes
bell			brick	
clarinet			cloth	
drum			glass	
drum sticks			leather	
flute			metal	
french horn			plastic	
guitar			string	
horn			thread	
keyboard			yarn	
maraca				
oboe				
organ				
party horn				
piano				
saxophone				
tambourine				
triangle				
trombone				
trumpet				
tuba				
violin				
xylophone				

Other Items

Structure	Notes		Notes
bridge			
chimney			
dumpster			
elevator			
escalator			
fence			
fire escape			
fire place			
gate			
lock			
roof			
side			
socket			
stairs			
steps			
window			

Other Items

Tool	Notes
broom	
cart	
chain	
chainsaw	
drill	
dustpan	
fire extinguisher	
flashlight	
gun	
hammer	
hoe	
hose	
ladder	
lawnmower	
mop	
nail	
net	
nut	
pipe	
pliers	
rake	
roller	
rope	
saw	
screw	
screw driver	
shovel	
thimble	
watering can	
wrench	

Travel	Notes
bags	
boat	
car seat	
cruise	
drivers license	
luggage	
luggage cart	
map	
passport	
plane	
seat belt	
suitcase	
train	

Outside

Body of Water	Notes	Land	Notes
bay		canyon	
brook		cliff	
creek		desert	
lake		field	
ocean		glacier	
pond		hill	
river		iceberg	
spring		island	
stream		mountain	
swap		valley	
waterfall		volcano	

Outside

Nature	Notes		Outer Space	Notes
acorn			astronaut	
beehive			earth	
cactus			mars	
clover			moon	
dirt			planet	
fire			satellite	
flower			space helmet	
fountain			space ship	
garden			space shuttle	
grass			space suit	
hay			star	
heat			sun	
icicle			telescope	
leaf			world	
log				
mud				
nest				
orchard				
palm tree				
pinecone				
plant				
rock				
sand				
seashell				
shadow				
sky				
smoke				
space				
spider web				
stick				
stone				
sunrise				
sunset				
tree				

Outside

Outside Thing	Notes	Weather	Notes
air		clear	
cross		cloud	
crosswalk		cloudy	
doghouse		cold	
fence		cool	
fire hydrant		dew	
fireworks		drizzle	
flag		flood	
float		fog	
foot print		freezing	
garden		frost	
gas		hail	
gas pump		hazy	
grill		hot	
ground		humid	
hole		hurricane	
lantern		ice	
lawn		icicle	
litter		lightning	
mailbox		mist	
path		puddle	
pole		rain	
post		rainbow	
railroad tracks		snow	
rainbow		snowflake	
road		sprinkle	
saddle		steamy	
sidewalk		storm	
snowman		sunshine	
street		temperature	
teepee		thunder	
tent		tornado	
traffic		warm	
traffic light		windy	
tree			
USA flag			
weather			
woods			

People

Family	Notes		People	Notes
aunt			adult	
brother			audience	
cousin			baby	
dad			boy	
father			bride	
godfather			child	
godmother			children	
grandchild			crowd	
grandchildren			friend	
granddaughter			girl	
grandma			groom	
grandpa			kid	
grandson			lady	
great grandma			man	
great grandpa			neighbor	
husband			people	
mom			person	
mother			woman	
nephew				
niece				
parent				
sister				
uncle				
wife				

People

Worker	Notes	Worker	Notes
actor		pilot	
artist		plumber	
anchorman		policeman	
astronaut		priest	
babysitter		principal	
baker		receptionist	
bank teller		sailor	
bus driver		scientist	
butcher		security guard	
carpenter		soldier	
cashier		teacher	
cheer leader		truck driver	
chef		TV reporter	
clerk		vet	
clown		waiter	
coach		waitress	
conductor		zoo keeper	
construction worker			
cowboy			
dancer			
dentist			
doctor			
eye doctor			
farmer			
fire fighter			
fisherman			
garbage man			
graduate			
hair stylist			
janitor			
jockey			
librarian			
life guard			
mailman			
mechanic			
minister			
musician			
nun			
nurse			
park ranger			
photographer			

Place

Place	Notes	Place	Notes
airport terminal		post office	
animal hospital		ranch	
backyard		restaurant	
ball park		runway	
ball pit		school	
bank		shed	
barn		skate park	
baseball field		skyscraper	
beach		soccer field	
building		street	
cabin		suburb	
camp		synagogue	
car wash		tennis court	
carnival		theater	
castle		town	
church		town hall	
city		toy store	
drive thru		train station	
dump		upstairs	
farm		waiting room	
fire station		water tower	
gas station		windmill	
grocery store			
harbor			
home			
hospital			
hotel			
house			
library			
lighthouse			
mall			
mosque			
motel			
museum			
office building			
park			
path			
playland			
playground			
police station			
pool			
porch			

Place

Play Area	Notes		Restaurant	Notes
amusement park			Applebee's	
ball pit			Arby's	
basketball court			Burger King	
beach			Chili's	
bouncy			Chinese Food	
carnival			Denny's	
jungle gym			Diner	
merry go round			Domino's Pizza	
monkey bars			Friendly's	
picnic table			KFC	
playland			Kmart	
pool			Krispy Kreme	
sandbox			McDonalds	
see saw			Pizza Hut	
slide			Starbucks	
swing			Steak House	
teeter totter			Subway	
tennis court			Subway	
tire swing			Taco Bell	
			Wendy's	

Place

School	Notes	School	Notes
backpack		school	
book		scissors	
calculator		snack	
calendar		stapler	
cartoon		story	
chair		table	
chalk		tape	
chalk board		teacher's desk	
classroom		water bottle	
coat hook		white board	
colored pencils			
computer			
crayon			
cubby			
desk			
easel			
envelope			
eraser			
globe			
glue			
juice box			
knapsack			
locker			
lunch box			
magazine			
mail			
marker			
monitor			
mouse			
notebook			
pad			
page			
paint			
paintbrush			
paper			
paper clip			
pen			
pencil			
pencil sharpener			
ruler			
schedule			

Place

Store	Notes		Notes
Barnes and Noble			
Bed, Bath & Beyond			
Blockbuster			
Department			
Hollywood Video			
JCPenney			
Kinko's			
KMart			
Macy			
Nordstrom			
Office Depot			
Payless Shoes			
Rite Aid			
Safeway			
Sears			
Staples			
Supercuts			
Supermarket			
Target			
Walgreens			
Walmart			

Play

Game	Notes		Toy	Notes
Bingo			ball	
Candyland			balloon	
Checkers			blocks	
Chess			bubbles	
Chutes & Ladders			cards	
Go Fish			castle	
Hide and Seek			clay	
Hopscotch			doll	
I Spy			doll house	
Lotto			doodle board	
Marbles			Duplos	
Memory			felt people	
Red Light - Green Light			jump rope	
Ring Around the Rosie			kite	
Scrabble			koosh balls	
Simon Says			Legos	
Tag			lincoln logs	
Tic Tac Toe			lotto	
			magnets	
			marbles	
			memory game	
			Mr.Potato Head	
			paints	
			Play Doh	
			playhouse	
			puzzle	
			shape sorter	
			stack beads	
			stencil	
			sticker	
			tinker toys	
			train track	
			trains	

Play

Story Character	Notes
angel	
devil	
dragon	
dwarf	
elf	
ghost	
giant	
king	
monster	
prince	
princess	
queen	
santa	
witch	
wizard	

Nursery Rhyme	Notes
Baa, Baa, Black Sheep	
Georgie Porgie	
Hickory Dickory Dock	
Humpty Dumpty	
I'm a Little Teapot	
Itsy Bitsy Spider	
Jack and Jill	
Jack be Nimble	
Little Bo Peep	
Little Jack Horner	
Little Miss Muffet	
Mary Had a Little Lamb	
Mulberry Bush	
Old MacDonald	
One, Two, Buckle My Shoe	
Pat-A-Cake	
Pease Porridge	
Peter, Peter, Pumpkin-Eater	
Pop! Goes the Weasel	
Rock a Bye Baby	
Star Light, Star Bright	
This Old Man	
Twinkle, Twinkle, Little Star	

School

Alphabet	Notes	Color	Notes
A		beige	
B		black	
C		blue	
D		brown	
E		cream	
F		fuchsia	
G		gold	
H		green	
I		grey	
J		indigo	
K		ivory	
L		khaki	
M		magenta	
N		maroon	
O		olive	
P		orange	
Q		pink	
R		purple	
S		red	
T		silver	
U		tan	
V		teal	
W		turquoise	
X		violet	
Y		white	
Z		yellow	

School

Grammar	Notes	Math	Notes
adjective		add	
comma		ATM	
exclamation point		cash	
noun		check	
paragraph		coin	
period		coupon	
preposition		credit card	
pronoun		dime	
question		divide	
question mark		dollar	
sentence		dot	
statement		equals	
verbs		line	
word		math	
		minus	
		money	
		multiply	
		nickel	
		penny	
		plus	
		point	
		quarter	
		subtract	

School

Number	Notes
zero	
one	
two	
three	
four	
five	
six	
seven	
eight	
nine	
ten	
eleven	
twelve	
thirteen	
fourteen	
fifteen	
sixteen	
seventeen	
eighteen	
nineteen	
twenty	
first	
second	
third	
fourth	
fifth	
sixth	
seventh	
eight	
ninth	
tenth	

Shape	Notes
circle	
diamond	
heart	
hexagon	
octagon	
oval	
rectangle	
square	
star	
trapezoid	
triangle	

Sport

Baseball	Notes		Basketball	Notes
base			basket	
baseball			basketball	
baseball diamond			basketball player	
baseball field			center court	
bat			court	
batting helmet			foul	
cap			head band	
concessions			referee	
home run			shirt	
mitt			shorts	
shirt			socks	
shorts			throw	
socks			time out	
t-ball			uniform	
umpire			wrist band	
uniform				

46

Sport

Football	Notes		Soccer	Notes
cheerleader			center	
field			coach	
field goal			field	
flag			flag	
football			goal	
pass			goal line	
penalty			kick	
quarterback			pass	
referee			penalty	
Superbowl			player	
tackle			post	
team			punt	
tee			referee	
throw			soccer ball	
touch down			uniform	
			water bottle	

Sport

Sport	Notes	Equipment	Notes
bicycle		ball	
bowling		bat	
field hockey		bicycle	
figure skating		bow & arrow	
fishing		diving board	
golf		elbow pad	
gymnastics		fins	
hiking		fishing pole	
hockey		glove	
horse shoe		goggles	
ice skating		golf clubs	
ping pong		helmet	
polo		ice skates	
pool		kneepad	
racket ball		net	
roller skating		paddle	
rugby		puck	
sailing		racquet	
skateboarding		roller blades	
skydiver		sled	
soccer		snow shoes	
softball		soccer ball	
squash		surfboard	
tball		tennis racquet	
tennis		trampoline	
volleyball		trophy	
		volley ball	
		wrist guard	

Verbal Behavior Targets - A Tool to Teach Mands, Tacts and Intraverbals

48

Time

Day of Week	Notes		Month	Notes
Sunday			January	
Monday			February	
Tuesday			March	
Wednesday			April	
Thursday			May	
Friday			June	
Saturday			July	
			August	
			September	
			October	
			November	
			December	

Time

Season	Notes		Time of Day	Notes
winter			1:00	
spring			2:00	
summer			3:00	
fall			4:00	
			5:00	
			6:00	
			7:00	
			8:00	
			9:00	
			10:00	
			11:00	
			12:00	
			after	
			afternoon	
			again	
			already	
			always	
			am	
			before	
			day	
			evening	
			hour	
			later	
			midnight	
			minute	
			morning	
			never	
			night	
			noon	
			now	
			once	
			pm	
			sometime	
			today	
			tomorrow	
			tonight	
			week	
			year	
			yesterday	

Vehicle

Aircraft	Notes	Boat	Notes
airplane		barge	
blimp		boat	
cockpit		bumper boat	
glider		canoe	
helicopter		catamaran	
hot air balloon		cruise liner	
jet		ferry	
parachute		fishing boat	
rocket ship		jet ski	
plane		kayak	
space shuttle		lifeboat	
		navy boat	
		raft	
		rowboat	
		sailboat	
		ship	
		speed boat	
		submarine	
		tug boat	
		windsurfer	

Vehicle

Land	Notes		Notes
ambulance			
bicycle			
bike			
bulldozer			
bus			
cab			
camper			
car			
carriage			
cement mixer			
digger			
dump truck			
fire truck			
garbage truck			
golf cart			
jeep			
motorcycle			
police car			
scooter			
shopping cart			
skateboard			
snow plow			
stroller			
SUV			
tank			
taxi			
tow truck			
tractor			
train			
tricycle			
trike			
trolley			
truck			
van			
wagon			
wheelchair			

Verb Set 1

Verb	Notes	Verb	Notes
bake		hop	
bark		hug	
blink		jump	
blow		kick	
bounce		kiss	
break		knock	
bring		laugh	
brush		match	
build		move	
button		open	
buy		paint	
carry		pee	
catch		play	
chase		point	
clap		poop	
clean		pour	
climb		pull	
close		push	
color		read	
comb		ride	
come		run	
cook		see	
cough		sing	
count		sit	
cover		sleep	
crash		slide	
crawl		sneeze	
cry		spill	
cut		stand	
dance		stomp	
dig		sleep	
draw		swim	
dress		swing	
drink		throw	
drive		tickle	
dry		walk	
eat		want	
fly		wash	
go		wave	
help			
hit			

Verb Set 2

Verb	Notes		Verb	Notes
act			love	
ask			make	
bat			mix	
beat			mow	
bite			name	
burn			order	
burp			pat	
change			pedal	
chop			peel	
dive			pet	
drop			pick	
dump			pinch	
erase			pound	
excuse			pretend	
fall			put	
feed			quit	
find			race	
finish			rain	
fish			rip	
fit			roll	
fix			say	
float			scratch	
flush			scrub	
fold			shake	
follow			shave	
get			shovel	
give			sip	
hand			skate	
have			smell	
hear			smile	
hide			splash	
hold			stop	
iron			touch	
itch			try	
juggle			wipe	
keep			work	
like			wrestle	
listen			write	
live			yawn	
look			zip	

Verb Set 3

Verb	Notes	Verb	Notes
add		share	
belong		shine	
bend		shoot	
bleed		shop	
can		show	
charge		shut	
check		slip	
chew		snap	
choke		snore	
cool		snow	
crack		snuggle	
deliver		spell	
dial		spin	
dunk		spit	
exercise		spray	
feel		squeeze	
fight		squirt	
fill		stack	
hang		start	
kneel		stay	
leave		stir	
lick		stretch	
lie		suck	
lock		swallow	
march		take	
mark		talk	
mop		tape	
paddle		taste	
plug		tear	
pop		thank	
pump		tie	
punch		trip	
reach		turn	
rest		type	
ring		unlock	
roast		vacuum	
rock		wait	
scream		wake	
set		watch	
sew		wear	

Verb Set 4

Verb	Notes		Verb	Notes
am			remember	
are			save	
be			scare	
bet			should	
bless			slap	
bother			sneak	
call			spend	
could			step	
die			stink	
do			tease	
dream			tell	
fire			think	
forget			tip	
freeze			use	
gobble			wade	
got			was	
grab			waste	
grow			were	
guess			whip	
happen			whisper	
has			will	
hate			wind	
hope			wink	
hurry			would	
hush				
is				
kill				
know				
let				
lift				
lose				
marry				
meet				
miss				
park				
pay				
peek				
pray				
press				
raise				

Verb Set 5

Emotion	Notes		Interaction	Notes
angry			argue	
bored			complain	
confused			fight	
embarrassed			hide	
excited			hug	
frustrated			kiss	
happy			play	
hurt			share	
jealous			shout	
lonely			talk	
mad			tease	
nervous			work	
proud			yell	
sad				
scared				
scary				
shy				
sick				
silly				
sleepy				
surprised				
tired				
worried				

Adjective

Adjective	Notes	Adjective	Notes
afraid		friendly	
angry		front	
alone		frozen	
apart		full	
asleep		funny	
awake		furry	
backward		fuzzy	
bad		gentle	
beautiful		gigantic	
best		gorgeous	
better		gone	
big		good	
bored		great	
bright		grumpy	
broken		handsome	
busy		happy	
careful		hard	
chilly		healthy	
clean		heavy	
closed		high	
clumsy		horrible	
cold		hot	
cool		hungry	
crazy		hurt	
cute		itchy	
dangerous		jolly	
dark		just	
dead		kind	
different		large	
difficult		last	
dirty		lazy	
dizzy		late	
dry		light	
early		little	
easy		long	
empty		low	
even		mad	
fat		many	
favorite		mean	
fine			
flat			

Verbal Behavior Targets - A Tool to Teach Mands, Tacts and Intraverbals

Adjective

Adjective	Notes	Adjective	Notes
medium		sore	
melted		sorry	
messy		sour	
mighty		spotty	
middle		sticky	
mushy		still	
naked		stinky	
narrow		straight	
nasty		strange	
naughty		striped	
neat		strong	
new		stuck	
nice		stupid	
noisy		super	
odd		sweet	
old		tall	
only		tame	
open		tart	
poor		tender	
pretty		thin	
quiet		thirsty	
quick		tight	
rainy		tricky	
rare		tiny	
ratty		together	
right		tough	
rough		ugly	
round		upside down	
salty		very	
same		watery	
scary		warm	
scrawny		well	
scratchy		wet	
sharp		wide	
short		wonderful	
sick		wrong	
silly		yet	
skinny		young	
small		yucky	
smooth		yummy	
soft			

Adverb

Adverb	Notes	Adverb	Notes
afterward			
almost			
always			
badly			
carefully			
clearly			
closely			
completely			
daily			
early			
easily			
fast			
first			
happily			
honestly			
loudly			
never			
now			
often			
quickly			
quietly			
rarely			
really			
recently			
sadly			
slowly			
sometimes			
soon			
today			
tomorrow			
too			
totally			
usually			
very			
well			

Comparative

Comparative	Notes		Notes
angrier			
bigger			
cleaner			
closer			
colder			
darker			
farther			
faster			
greater			
happier			
heavier			
hotter			
larger			
lighter			
longer			
older			
sadder			
shorter			
slower			
smaller			
taller			
thinner			

Conjunction

Conjunction	Notes		Notes
after			
although			
and			
as			
because			
before			
but			
either			
for			
if			
neither			
or			
since			
so			
still			
than			
that			
then			
though			
till			
unless			
until			
while			

Preposition

Preposition	Notes		Preposition	Notes
about			up	
above			with	
across			without	
after				
against				
along				
around				
at				
away				
back				
before				
behind				
below				
beneath				
beside				
between				
bottom				
by				
down				
for				
forth				
from				
here				
in				
in back of				
in front of				
inside				
into				
near				
next to				
of				
off				
on				
on top of				
onto				
out of				
over				
there				
through				
to				
top				
under				

Pronoun

Pronoun	Notes
anybody	
anyone	
anything	
everybody	
everyone	
everything	
he	
her	
hers	
herself	
him	
himself	
his	
I	
it	
itself	
me	
mine	
my	
myself	
no one	
nobody	
nothing	
our	
ours	
ourselves	
she	
somebody	
someone	
something	
that	
their	
theirs	
them	
themselves	
these	
they	
this	
those	
us	

Pronoun	Notes
we	
you	
your	
yours	
yourself	
yourselves	

Quantifier

Quantifier	Notes		Notes
a lot of			
all			
also			
another			
any			
bit			
bite			
both			
bunch			
couple			
each			
else			
enough			
every			
few			
half			
least			
less			
lots of			
many			
more			
most			
much			
none			
other			
pair			
part			
piece			
plenty of			
rest			
several			
some			
whole			

Chapter 2

Multiple Words

This chapter provides categories of targets that are made of multiple words. A child can start to learn multiple words after building a vocabulary of a small set of functional words. Someone who has acquired a few mands using single words starts to understand that words can meet needs and wants. Multiple words are helpful to communicate needs that are more complicated. Most words are used in the context of other words, so learning words in common phrases is practical because a child will have frequent exposure in the natural environment to multiple word phrases.

Targets from multiple categories can be taught simultaneously. Different targets should be selected to satisfy the interests and needs of each individual. Fill-in-the-blank phrases, songs, animal sounds, and verb/noun pairs can be practiced in various educational and natural settings. Numerous opportunities to imitate phrases and use words functionally in relevant settings should be arranged for the child.

Fill in the blank phrases can be practiced in natural settings. While playing on a swing you can say "ready, set, go". After saying the phrase multiple times, you can say "ready, set, ___" and wait for the child to say "go". Sounds of animals and objects can be incorporated into fun activities. For example, you can play with a toy cow and make the sound "moo" and have the child imitate you. Then say "a cow says ____" or "What says moo?"

Songs can be sung in many settings. Lyrics from songs can be used for fill in the blank phrases. The chorus in a song offers the opportunity to sing a phrase and have the child imitate the same phrase. Songs are delivered in a different tone of voice that may be soothing, pleasant, and appealing to a child.

Word Association

Fill in the Blank	Notes	Noun and Noun	Notes
blow your nose		bacon and eggs	
brush your teeth		ball and glove	
clap your hands		bat and ball	
clean up the mess		boy and girl	
close your eyes		bread and butter	
don't fall down		brush and paint	
drink your juice		cake and ice cream	
drive the car		candles and cake	
dry your hands		cheese and crackers	
feed the dog		circle and triangle	
finish your work		comb and brush	
fly a kite		glove and hand	
gobble you up		hammer and nail	
going to get you		hat and coat	
good bye		king and queen	
hang up your coat		knife and fork	
knock, knock		milk and cookies	
lay down in bed		moon and stars	
listen to music		mother and father	
one, two, three		pancakes and syrup	
open the door		peanut butter and jelly	
peek-a-boo		pencil and paper	
pet the dog		pillow and bed	
pull up your pants		ring and finger	
push the button		salt and pepper	
raise your hand		shovel and pail	
ready set go		socks and shoes	
run for your life		spider and web	
sing a song		table and chair	
stomp your feet		toothbrush and toothpaste	
take off your shoes		train and track	
this little piggy			
tie your shoes			
time for bed			
turn on the TV			
wash your hands			
wipe your nose			

Word Association

Opposite	Notes	Opposite	Notes
all - none		push - pull	
alone - together		short - long	
asleep - awake		sit - stand	
before - after		slow - fast	
beginning - end		soft - hard	
big - little		stop - go	
black - white		thin - thick	
broken - fixed		tiny - huge	
clean - dirty		top - bottom	
come - go		true - false	
day - night		up - down	
dead - alive		wet - dry	
empty - full		yes - no	
first - last			
flat - bumpy			
friend - enemy			
front - back			
get - give			
good - bad			
hairy - bald			
happy - sad			
he - she			
heavy - light			
help - hurt			
hot - cold			
hungry - stuffed			
in - out			
large - small			
late - early			
laugh - cry			
lazy - working			
light - dark			
loose - tight			
make - destroy			
man - woman			
man - women			
many - few			
messy - neat			
old - new			
on - off			
open - closed			

Word Association

Song	Notes
A-Tisket, a-Tasket	
Ba Ba Black Sheep	
Bingo	
Down by the Station	
Frere Jacques	
Head Shoulders Knees and Toes	
Hey Diddle Diddle	
Hickory Dickory Dock	
Hokey Pokey	
How much is that Doggie?	
If You're Happy And You Know It	
Itsy Bitsy Spider	
I've Been Working On The Railroad	
John Jacob Jingle Heimer Schmidt	
Little Bo Peep	
London Bridges	
Mary Had A Little Lamb	
Michael Row Your Boat Ashore	
Oh Dear What Can The Matter Be?	
Oh Susanna	
Old MacDonald Had A Farm	
Pop Goes The Weasel	
Ring Around The Rosie	
Row, Row, Row Your Boat	
She'll Be Coming Around The Mountain	
The Ants Go Marching	
The Bear Went Over The Mountain	
The More We Get Together	
The Muffin Man	
The Wheels On The Bus	
This Little Light of Mine	
This Little Piggy Went to Market	
This Old Man	
Three Blind Mice	
Twinkle, Twinkle Little Star	

Word Association

Sound - Animal	Notes	Sound - Object	Notes
bee -- buzz		baby -- wa wa	
bird -- tweet tweet		bubble – pop	
cat -- meow		car -- beep beep	
chicken -- cheep		clock -- tick tock	
cow -- moo		doorbell -- ding dong	
crow -- caw		drum -- boom boom	
dog -- woof woof		hands -- clap	
donkey --hee haw		horn -- honk	
duck -- quack		piano -- de da la	
frog -- ribbit		rain -- splish splash	
goat -- maaa		siren -- whoo whoo	
horse -- neigh		telephone -- ring	
lion -- roar		train -- choo choo	
mouse -- squeak		wipers -- swish	
owl -- hoo hoo			
pig -- oink			
rooster -- cock a doodle do			
sheep -- baa baa			
snake -- hiss			
turkey -- gobble			

Word Association

Synonym	Notes		Notes
after -- behind			
all -- every			
begin --start			
big -- large			
boy -- male			
buddy -- friend			
call -- shout			
car -- automobile			
close -- shut			
easy -- simple			
end -- finish			
girl -- female			
give -- hand			
go -- leave			
Keep-- hold			
kids -- children			
like--enjoy			
listen -- hear			
look -- see			
loud -- noisy			
make -- build			
mix -- stir			
night -- evening			
one -- single			
over -- above			
picture -- photo			
right -- correct			
small -- little			
take -- grab			
talk -- speak			

Communication

Functional	Notes	Functional	Notes
Bless you		Ready set go	
Come in		Stop it	
Come on		Thank you	
Do not		Thanks	
Don't do that		That one	
Excuse me		That's mine	
Finished		This one	
Get me		Tickle me	
Give me that		Watch out	
Go away			
Good job			
Help me			
Here I am			
I am sick			
I am sorry			
I am tired			
I can't wait			
I did it			
I don't care			
I don't know			
I don't like that			
I don't want to			
I'm all done			
I'm ready			
Is that ok?			
It's for you			
It's my turn			
Leave me alone			
Let me see			
Let's go			
Let's play			
Look at me			
Look at that			
Look out			
Move please			
My turn			
OK			
Over there			
Please			
Quiet			
Ready			

Communication

Greeting	Notes	Interjection	Notes
bye		cool	
goodbye		darn	
hello		hooray	
hey		oh	
hi		oh no	
see ya		ouch	
		owee	
		phooey	
		shoot	
		surprise	
		tah dah	
		uh oh	
		whoops	
		wow	
		yuk	
		yummy	

Communication

Expression	Notes	Yes or No	Notes
Another one		alright	
Anything else?		can't	
As soon as possible		couldn't	
By the way		don't	
Don't worry		no	
For example		no thanks	
Giddyup		not	
Go for it		okay	
Good idea		right	
Good luck		shouldn't	
Have a good day		sure	
Have a good time		won't	
Have in common		wouldn't	
I don't know		yes	
I have no idea			
I made a mistake			
I really mean it			
I see			
In a hurry			
In a little bit			
In the first place			
Inside out			
On the other hand			
Sick and tired			
Some more			
Take it easy			
That's a good idea			
That's fun			
That's great			
That's too bad			
That's weird			
There it goes			
Too high			
Too small			
Well			
You're right			
You're welcome			

Phrase

Color + Noun	Notes	Comment	Notes
black dog		I found a	
blue ball		I got a	
blue coat		I have a	
brown sock		I hear a	
green hat		I like to	
grey box		I need a	
orange crayon		I see a	
pink shoe		I smell a	
purple paper		I use a	
red shirt		I want a	
white lamp			
yellow bag			

Phrase

Noun + Location	Notes		Number + Noun	Notes
box under table			one shoe	
bridge over water			two bananas	
chair next to table			three carrots	
dog in house			four balls	
hat on head			five cookies	
keys behind book				
sign above door				
train off track				

Phrase

Of Phrase	Notes	Possessor + Possession	Notes
bag of chips		baby's bottle	
bag of popcorn		her dress	
bag of pretzels		his hat	
bag of toys		king's crown	
bar of soap		mom's car	
bottle of pills		my shoes	
bowl of cereal		my truck	
box of cereal		our house	
bunch of grapes		queen's castle	
can of soda		their game	
can of soup		your dog	
glass of milk			
head of lettuce			
loaf of bread			
pack of gum			
pair of boots			
pair of earrings			
pair of pants			
pair of shoes			
pair of skates			
pair of socks			
piece of bacon			
piece of cake			
scoop of ice cream			
sheet of paper			
slice of bread			
stick of butter			
tube of toothpaste			

Phrase

Pronoun + Verb	Notes
he drinks	
he eats	
she climbs	
she rides	
they run	
we swim	

Size + Noun	Notes
big dog	
big fire truck	
big piano	
big train	
huge elephat	
little ball	
little mouse	
small button	
small marshmallow	
tall giraffe	
tiny raisin	

Phrase

Verb + Noun	Notes	Verb + Noun	Notes
brush dog		get ball	
brush hair		get box	
brush teeth		get better	
carry bag		give coat	
carry box		give drink	
carry shoes		give socks	
clean fingernails		go to bathroom	
clean table		go to kitchen	
clean window		go to park	
close book		hit ball	
close box		hit balloon	
close container		hit table	
close door		hold baby	
cook bacon		hold rabbit	
cook meat		hold umbrella	
cook muffins		jump down	
cover bed		jump fence	
cover box		jump rope	
cover doll		kick ball	
draw circle		kick floor	
draw face		kick wall	
draw snowman		open box	
dress baby		open container	
dress boy		open door	
dress doll		open refrigerator	
drop ball		paint picture	
drop block		peel apple	
drop book		peel banana	
dry dishes		peel orange	
dry face		pet cat	
dry hands		pet dog	
eat banana		pet hamster	
eat cookie		pinch arm	
eat muffin		pinch leg	
feed baby		pinch nose	
feed cat		play cards	
feed horse		play cars	
fix car		play computer	
fix it		play games	
fix that		play house	
fix toy		play Wii	

80

Phrase

Verb + Noun	Notes
play drum	
play game	
play grocery	
play guitar	
play kitchen	
play piano	
play with beads	
point to door	
point to house	
point to oven	
pour juice	
pour milk	
pour tea	
pull chair	
pull train	
pull wagon	
push box	
push swing	
push wagon	
put in candy	
put in cookie	
put in money	
put on coat	
put on shirt	
put on shoes	
raise hand	
read book	
read map	
read paper	
ride bike	
ride horse	
ride train	
scratch arm	
scratch head	
scratch leg	
shake hand	
shake head	
shake tambourine	
sit on chair	
sit on couch	

Verb + Noun	Notes
sit on floor	
smell bacon	
smell chocolate	
smell flower	
take off coat	
take off hat	
take off shoes	
throw ball	
throw fit	
throw leaves	
touch feet	
touch head	
touch nose	
wash face	
wash hands	
water flower	
water grass	
water plant	

Verbal Behavior Targets - A Tool to Teach Mands, Tacts and Intraverbals

Chapter 3

Instructions and Questions

This chapter contains instructions that a child can follow and questions to ask and answer. Simple instructions can be taught to a child early in their language program. For example, functional instructions like, "come here" and "don't touch that" are important for a child to understand in his natural environment. Instructions from multiple categories can be taught simultaneously, however, the advanced instructions require mastery of simple instructions first.

A variety of question types are provided along with many examples in each category. Questions that begin with what, who, and where are typically taught first. These beginning question types often have literal and easy to memorize answers that a child can learn and reproduce. The more advanced question types of how, when, which and why are introduced after the first three types of questions are mastered. However, you are encouraged to consult a language curriculum to help you make sequencing decisions and to choose targets based on what you know about your student's abilities and interests.

The "Ask Questions" category provides functional questions that a child can be taught to ask of other people. For example "Can I play?", "When can I go?", and "Where is it?" are useful questions for a child to ask. One of the most useful questions for a child to learn to ask is, "What's that?" Once a child can learn to ask questions for information instead of just to gain objects then he is likely to be able to learn more and engage more interactively with others.

82

Instructions

Body Function	Notes	Body Function	Notes
arm - raise		nose - snore	
arms - wave		toes - wiggle	
bottom - sit on		tongue - lick	
ears - hear		tongue - stick out	
ears - listen		tongue - taste	
elbows - bend		nose - sneeze	
eyes - blink			
eyes - close			
eyes - look			
eyes - open			
eyes - see			
feet - hop			
feet - jump			
feet - run			
feet - stomp			
feet - tap			
feet - walk			
fingernails - cut			
fingers - point			
fingers - tap			
fingers - wiggle			
hair - brush			
hair - comb			
hair - cut			
hair - wash			
hands - clap			
hands - wash			
hands - wave			
knees - bend			
legs - jump			
legs - run			
legs - skip			
legs - walk			
lips - blow			
lips – kiss			
lips - pucker			
lips - whistle			
mouth - eat			
mouth - smile			
mouth - talk			
nose - blow			

Instructions

Situational	Notes	Object Use	Notes
Come here		Blow bubbles	
Don't touch that		Blow the whistle	
Give me that		Build a tower	
Go over to X		Eat the pizza	
Hug		Fly the airplane	
Jump		Hit the drum	
Pick up		Hug the doll	
Point to the X		Kiss the bear	
Put that down		Open the book	
Raise arm		Play xylophone	
Run		Push the wagon	
Sit down		Put on the hat	
Stand up		Shake the tambourine	
Stomp your feet		Talk on the telephone	
Stop that		Throw the ball	
Touch your head		Put the blocks away	
Wave bye bye			
Wipe your mouth			

Instructions

Fine Motor	Notes
Blow a kiss	
Clap	
Give me 5	
Jump	
Nod your head	
Raise your arm	
Shake your leg	
Stomp your feet	
Stretch your arms	
Tap the table	
Thumbs up	
Touch your toes	
Wiggle your fingers	

Discrimination	Notes
Cover the	
Find the	
Get the	
Give me	
Hand the	
Let go of	
Name a	
Open the	
Pick up	
Point to	
Shake the	
Show me	
Take one	
Tell me	
Touch the	

Instructions

Gross Motor	Notes	Pretend	Notes
Bend your knees		Be a cat	
Close the door		Be a dog	
Go sit in the corner		Be a lion	
Go to the bathroom		Be a monster	
Hop on one foot		Blow your nose	
Knock on the table		Brush teeth	
Lay down		Brush your hair	
Put this in the box		Draw a picture	
Reach for the sky		Drink the water	
Throw this away		Drive the car	
Touch the wall		Eat a cookie	
Turn around		Fly an airplane	
Turn on the light		Go to sleep	
Wash your hands		Ride the horse	
Wave the book		Talk on the telephone	

Instructions

Advanced Instruction	Notes
Find dad and give him this note	
Give me A and cover B	
Give me A and put the B in the Y	
Give me A, B, and C	
Give the A to X and put the B on the Y	
Go give this to mom in the kitchen	
Go to named person and get an object	
Go to the bathroom and get the book	
Go to the kitchen and get the chips	
Pick up A and put down B	
Pick up the box and put it on the table	
Put the X on the Y and the A under the B	
Shake the X, put it on top of the Y, and close the door	
Shake X and put B in the Y	
Touch the wall and go to the chair	
Wave the paper and then throw it down	

Question

Ask Question	Notes
Are you going?	
Are you ok?	
Can I go?	
Can I have a turn?	
Can I have a X?	
Can I have that?	
Can I play?	
Can I stay?	
Can I take a break?	
Do you want this?	
Does this one fit?	
Does this one work?	
How are you?	
How do I use it?	
How do you do it?	
How does it work?	
How many are there?	
Is there a show on?	
Is this your cup?	
What are you doing?	
What can you do?	
What color?	
What did you do?	
What did you say?	
What did you see?	
What do you drink?	
What do you eat?	
What do you have?	
What do you like?	
What do you want?	
What does he eat?	
What does he say?	
What happened?	
What is it?	
What is that?	
What is this for?	
What is your name?	
What should I do?	
What time is it?	
What's he doing?	
What's in the box?	
What's that?	

Question

Ask Question	Notes
What's wrong?	
When can I eat?	
When can I go?	
When can I have that?	
Where are the X?	
Where are you going?	
Where are you?	
Where can I get more of these?	
Where does it go?	
Where did you go?	
Where do you find it?	
Where do you put this?	
Where does he live?	
Where is X?	
Where is he?	
Where is it?	
Which one can I have?	
Which one is mine?	
Which one?	
Who has it?	
Who has the X?	
Who is that?	
Who uses this?	
Who's there?	
Whose is this?	
Whose turn is it?	
Why do I have to?	
Why does it work?	
Why?	
Will you fix this?	

Question

Academic	Notes
What are bodies of water?	
What are cities?	
What are coins?	
What are community helpers?	
What are continents?	
What are days of the week?	
What are dinosaurs?	
What are forest plants?	
What are habitats?	
What are holiday?	
What are months?	
What are planets?	
What are some natural disasters?	
What are some states?	
What are some traffic signs?	
What are the seasons?	
What are types of weather?	
What are water animals?	
Where are land forms?	
Where are places to live?	
Who is in a family?	
Who is the president?	

Question

Community	Notes
Do you walk on the road?	
What do we do at Target?	
What do you do at the gas station?	
What do you do at Costco?	
What do you get at Blockbuster?	
What do you see at the airport?	
What is at the beach?	
What is at the grocery store?	
What is at the library?	
What is at the park?	
What is at the playground?	
What is at the post office?	
What is in the backyard?	
What is in the forest?	
What restaurant do you like?	
When do you see fireworks?	
Where do you like to go?	
Where does mail go?	
Where is your school?	
Who is at the fire station?	
Who is at the police station?	
Who is the president?	
Why do you see a fire truck?	

Question

Current Event	Notes
Did you see X?	
How is the weather?	
What are you watching?	
What do you do at a Birthday party?	
What do you do at Halloween?	
What do you do at night time?	
What do you do at Thanksgiving?	
What do you do in the afternoon?	
What do you do in the morning?	
What do you do in the snow?	
What do you do on Sunday?	
What do you want for your birthday?	
What happens at a baseball game?	
What happens at Easter?	
What happens on Christmas?	
What happens on New Years eve?	
What happens on the 4th of July?	

Question

How	Notes
How do birds fly?	
How do you blow out candles?	
How do you bounce a ball?	
How do you brush your teeth?	
How do you buy things?	
How do you check out a library book?	
How do you comb your hair?	
How do you cook food?	
How do you cut meat?	
How do you cut paper?	
How do you cut wood?	
How do you draw a face?	
How do you dry your hair?	
How do you dry your hands?	
How do you eat a banana?	
How do you eat an orange?	
How do you eat cereal?	
How do you eat dinner?	
How do you fly a kite?	
How do you get dressed?	
How do you get to school?	
How do you glue things together?	
How do you go down a slide?	
How do you go swimming?	
How do you go to sleep?	
How do you go up a slide?	
How do you hit a nail?	
How do you keep your hands warm?	
How do you keep your head warm?	
How do you kick a ball?	
How do you mail a letter?	
How do you make a sand castle?	
How do you make a sandwich?	
How do you make applesauce?	
How do you measure something?	
How do you open a present?	
How do you play a drum?	
How do you play a guitar?	
How do you play the piano?	
How do you put on shoes?	
How do you ride a bike?	
How do you stop the rain on your head?	

Question

How	Notes
How do you take a bath?	
How do you tell time?	
How do you trim your nails?	
How do you unlock the door?	
How do you wash your hair?	
How do you wash your hands?	
How do you watch TV?	
How do you jump?	
How do you talk quietly?	

Question

Personal Event	Notes
What did you do at school?	
What did you do yesterday?	
What did you eat for breakfast?	
What do you do at the beach?	
What do you do at the playground?	
What do you like to do?	
What do you want for Christmas?	
What do you want for your birthday?	
What do you want to do tomorrow?	
What will you be for Halloween?	
Where do you play?	

Question

Social	Notes
Do you have a bike?	
Do you have a brother?	
Do you have a pet?	
Do you have a sister?	
Do you like broccoli?	
Do you like candy?	
Do you want this one or that one?	
Do you wear glasses?	
How are you doing?	
How old are you?	
What are you doing?	
What are you playing with?	
What are you eating?	
What color are your eyes?	
What color is mom's car?	
What color is your hair?	
What do you have?	
What do you like to do?	
What do you like to drink?	
What do you like to eat?	
What is your address?	
What is your favorite book?	
What is your favorite movie?	
What is your last name?	
What is your name?	
What is your pet?	
What is your phone number?	
When is your birthday?	
Where do you go to school?	
Where do you live?	
Where were you born?	
Who cuts your hair?	
Who is your brother?	
Who is your cousin?	
Who is your dad?	
Who is your favorite?	
Who is your friend?	
Who is your mom?	
Who is your neighbor?	
Who is your sister?	
Who is your teacher?	

Question

When	Notes
When do flowers bloom? - in spring	
When do leaves turn color? - in the fall	
When do you answer the phone? - rings	
When do you bleed? - get a cut	
When do you clean up? - done playing	
When do you close your eyes? - sleep	
When do you comb your hair? - messy	
When do you cover your mouth? - cough	
When do you cry? - sad	
When do you drink? - thirsty	
When do you dry off? - after a bath	
When do you eat breakfast? - morning	
When do you eat dinner? - night time	
When do you eat? - hungry	
When do you eat a snack? – after school	
When do you fly a kite? - its windy	
When do you get dressed? - naked	
When do you get quiet? - to listen	
When do you go to the beach? - summer	
When do you hurry? - late	
When do you laugh? - get tickled	
When do you laugh? - something is funny	
When do you need a bowl? - eat cereal	
When do you need a broom? - sweep floor	
When do you need a mop? - wash the floor	
When do you open the door? - go outside	
When do you put on a Band-Aid? - cut skin	
When do you put on socks? - feet are cold	
When do you say goodbye? - leave	
When do you say hello? - meet someone	
When do you say please? - ask for things	
When do you scratch? - itchy	
When do you sit down? - tired of standing	
When do you sleep? - tired	
When do you smile? - happy	
When do you snore? - sleep	
When do you splash? - in the water	
When do you take a bath? - at night time	
When do you take medicine? – you're sick	
When do you turn on light? – it's dark	
When do you turn on the fan? - too hot	

Question

When	Notes
When do you turn pages? - read a book	
When do you use a hairdryer? -wet hair	
When do you use a key? - door is locked	
When do you use a shovel? - to dig	
When do you use a tissue? - blow nose	
When do you use an umbrella? - rains	
When do you use blocks? - to build tower	
When do you use scissors? - to cut paper	
When do you shampoo? - hair is dirty	
When do you wake up? - morning	
When do you wash? - dirty	
When do you water the grass? - summer	
When do you wear a coat? - winter	
When do you wear a costume? - Halloween	
When do you wear a hat? - winter	
When do you wear a seatbelt? - in car	
When do you wear sunglasses? - sunny	
When do you yell? - angry	
When does it snow? - in winter	
When does the sun rise? - morning	
When does the sun set? - night time	
When does your hair blow? - it's windy	
When is your TV show on? - varies	
When should you clean the table? - after dinner	
When should you cut your fingernails? - too long	
When should you go to school? - Mon - Fri	
When should you look both ways? - cross the street	
When should you make your bed? - get up	
When should you turn off a light? - leave the room	
When should you use a fork? - to eat	
When should you use a napkin? - eat	
When should you use a tissue? - to blow your nose	

Question

Where	Notes
Where are the clouds? - sky	
Where are the stars? - sky	
Where are your fingers? - hand	
Where are your pillows? - bed	
Where do airplanes land? - airport	
Where do ants live? - dirt	
Where do cars drive? - traffic	
Where do fish live? - water	
Where do fire engines go? - fire station	
Where do monkeys live? - jungle	
Where do oranges grow? - orange tree	
Where do people pray? - church	
Where do people ski? - on snow	
Where do pumpkins grow? - pumpkin patch	
Where do trains stop? - train station	
Where do you bake muffins? - oven	
Where do you borrow books? - library	
Where do you build a snowman? - snow	
Where do you buy books? - bookstore	
Where do you buy food? - grocery store	
Where do you buy fries? - McDonalds	
Where do you buy shoes? - shoe store	
Where do you buy toys? - toy store	
Where do you eat food? - kitchen	
Where do you find a bed? - bedroom	
Where do you find a blanket? - bed	
Where do you find a roof? - house	
Where do you find a toilet? - bathroom	
Where do you find hair? - head	
Where do you find sand? - beach	
Where do you find wings? - bird	
Where do you golf? - golf course	
Where is a can opener? - kitchen	
Where do you get gas? - gas station	
Where do you get mail? - mailbox	
Where do you get money? - bank	
Where do you get sunburned? - skin	
Where do you slide? - at the park	
Where do you go to eat? - restaurant	
Where do you go shopping? - store	
Where do you have a zipper? - pants	

Question

Where	Notes
Where do you jump in the water? - pool	
Where do you keep a hamster? - cage	
Where do you keep eggs? - refrigerator	
Where does food stay cold? - refrigerator	
Where do you keep your bicycle? - garage	
Where do you park a car? - garage	
Where do you play computer? - office	
Where do you play in the sand? - sand box	
Where do you put a CD? - computer	
Where do you put a DVD? - DVD player	
Where do you put cheese? - pizza	
Where do chocolate chips go? -cookies	
Where do you put coffee? - mug	
Where do you put dirty clothes? - washer	
Where do you put a leash? - dog	
Where do you put the mail? - mailbox	
Where do you put raisins? - muffins	
Where do you put shampoo? - hair	
Where do you put your coat? - closet	
Where does your head go at night? - pillow	
Where do you run around? - park	
Where do you sit? - chair	
Where do you sleep? - bed	
Where do you stay on vacation? - motel	
Where do you swim? - pool	
Where do you take a walk? - outside	
Where do you use a lawn mower? - grass	
Where do you use a tent? - forest	
Where do you warm up food? - microwave	
Where do you wash your hands? - sink	
Where do you wear a hat? - head	
Where do you wear a seatbelt? - car	
Where do you wear glasses? - eyes	
Where do you wear pants? - legs	
Where do people work? - office	
Where does a bird sleep? - nest	
Where does a cow live? - farm	
Where does a dog live? - house	
Where does a frog live? - pond	
Where does a horse sleep? - barn	
Where does a leaf grow? - tree	
Where does an astronaut go? - space	

Question

Where	Notes
Where does an elephant live? - jungle	
Where does daylight come from? - sun	
Where does it snow? - outside	
Where does Pooh live? - 100 Acre Wood	
Where does Tarzan live? - jungle	
Where is the dishwasher? - kitchen	
Where is the dryer? - laundry room	
Where is the oven? - kitchen	
Where is the refrigerator? - kitchen	
Where is the shower? - bathroom	
Where is the sink? - bathroom	
Where is the toilet? - bathroom	
Where is the TV? - family room	
Where is your belly button? - belly	
Where is your ear? - head	
Where is your hair? - head	
Where is your hand? - arm	
Where is your knee? - leg	
Where is your nose? - face	
Where is your toothbrush? - bathroom	

Question

Which	Notes
Which is a food? - cake or tree	
Which is a plant? - tree or shoe	
Which is an animal? - dog or book	
Which is an insect? - butterfly or train	
Which is big? - elephant or mouse	
Which is blue? - sky or stars	
Which is cold? - snow or scissors	
Which is green? - grass or dirt	
Which is hot? - sun or snow	
Which is little? - bug or cow	
Which is pretty? - flower or dirt	
Which is salty? - chips or cake	
Which is sour? - lemon or cookie	
Which is sweet? - candy or chips	
Which is wet? - water or car	
Which is white? - cloud or grass	
Which one comes in a bunch? - grapes or meat	
Which one cries? - baby or pencil	
Which one do you blow? - bubbles or tape	
Which one do you catch? - ball or couch	
Which one do you clean up? - room or telephone	
Which one do you crack? - egg or chair	
Which one do you drink from? - cup or plate	
Which one do you eat with? - mouth or legs	
Which one do you eat? - cookie or chair	
Which one do you fly in? - airplane or train	
Which one do you hear with? - ears or hands	
Which one do you kick with? - foot or hand	
Which one do you live in? - house or computer	
Which one do you look in? - mirror or ball	
Which one do you peel? - banana or hot dog	
Which one do you play? - piano or pants	
Which one do you push? - wagon or house	
Which one do you put in the VCR? – video/ book	
Which one do you read? - book or camera	
Which one do you ride? - bike or chair	
Which one do you see with? - eyes or feet	
Which one do you sit on? - chair or TV	
Which one do you sleep in? - bed or bathtub	
Which one do you smell with? - nose or hair	
Which one do you swim in? - pool or sink	
Which one do you turn on? - TV or book	

Question

Which	Notes
Which one do you wash in? - bathtub or oven	
Which one do you watch? - TV or pencil	
Which one do you wear? - shoes or bed	
Which one eats? - cow or bike	
Which one has leaves? - tree or grass	
Which one has pages? - book or video	
Which one writes? - pencil or scissors	
Which one do you swim in? - pool or sink	
Which one do you use to touch? - hands or knees	

Question

Who	Notes
Who builds a house? - carpenter	
Who catches fish? - fisherman	
Who cleans up? - janitor	
Who cleans your teeth? - dentist	
Who cooks food? - chef	
Who cries? - baby	
Who cuts meat? - butcher	
Who dances? - dancer	
Who delivers mail? - mailman	
Who do you play with? - kids	
Who drives a bus? - bus driver	
Who drives a train? - conductor	
Who eats bananas? - monkey	
Who eats grass? - horse	
Who eats honey? - bear	
Who feels happy? - clown	
Who fights fires? - fireman	
Who fixes cars? - mechanic	
Who fixes pipes? - plumber	
Who flies an airplane? - pilot	
Who flies in space? - astronaut	
Who flies? - bird	
Who guards the pool? - lifeguard	
Who has a long tail? - monkey	
Who has big ears? - elephant	
Who has black stripes? - zebra	
Who has long neck? - giraffe	
Who has whiskers? - cat	
Who helps a sick person? - doctor	
Who helps people? - policeman	
Who helps you at the library? - librarian	
Who hops? - bunny	
Who is a bear? - Pooh	
Who is a big animal? - elephant	
Who is a dog? - Spot	
Who is a dwarf? - Sneezy	
Who is a girl? - Madeline	
Who is a jungle man? - Tarzan	
Who is a little animal? - rabbit	
Who is a man? - Dad	
Who is a princess? - Snow White	
Who is a woman? - Mom	

Verbal Behavior Targets - A Tool to Teach Mands, Tacts and Intraverbals

Question

Who	Notes
Who is scary? - monster	
Who juggles balls? - juggler	
Who kicks the ball? - soccer player	
Who leads circle time? - teacher	
Who leaps? - frog	
Who lives in a castle? - king	
Who lives in the White House?- president	
Who lives next door? - neighbor	
Who makes you laugh? - clown	
Who plants food? - farmer	
Who plays baseball? - baseball player	
Who plays basketball? - basketball player	
Who plays music? - musician	
Who pulls a wagon? - horse	
Who purrs? - cat	
Who rides a broom? - witch	
Who rides a horse? - cowboy	
Who stinks? - skunk	
Who swims in the water? - fish	
Who swings a bat? - baseball player	
Who takes the garbage? - garbage man	
Who throws a football? - football player	
Who watches kids? - babysitter	
Who wears a crown? - king	
Who works at a restaurant? - waitress	
Who works at the store? - cashier	
Who works at the zoo? - zoo keeper	
Who sails a boat? - sailor	

Question

Why	Notes
Why do babies cry?	
Why do you brush your teeth?	
Why do you button a shirt?	
Why do you cook food?	
Why do you cover your mouth when you cough?	
Why do you drink water?	
Why do you drive a car?	
Why do you eat cake?	
Why do you eat food?	
Why do you get gas?	
Why do you go to a restaurant?	
Why do you go to school?	
Why do you go to the doctor?	
Why do you go to the zoo?	
Why do you peel a banana?	
Why do you put away Play Doh?	
Why do you put cereal in a bowl?	
Why do you raise your hand?	
Why do you sleep?	
Why do you stop at a red light?	
Why do you tie a string on a balloon?	
Why do you use a backpack?	
Why do you use a blanket?	
Why do you use a fishing pole?	
Why do you use a knife?	
Why do you use a ladder?	
Why do you use a napkin?	
Why do you use a pencil?	
Why do you use a telephone?	
Why do you use a tissue?	
Why do you use a towel?	
Why do you use a washing machine?	
Why do you use an umbrella?	
Why do you use ice?	
Why do you use inside voices?	
Why do you use lights?	
Why do you use silverware?	
Why do you use soap?	
Why do you use the stairs?	
Why do you walk by the pool?	
Why do you wash your hands?	

Question

Why	Notes
Why do you water plants?	
Why do you wear a bathing suit?	
Why do you wear a coat?	
Why do you wear a watch?	
Why do you wear boots?	
Why do you wear glasses?	
Why do you wear sandals?	
Why does a building have a door?	
Why does a house have a window?	

Question

Yes or No	Notes
Can a fish sleep in a bed?	
Can a fish swim?	
Can a horse say neigh?	
Can a horse sit in a chair?	
Can a lion roar?	
Can a lion take a shower?	
Can a zebra brush his teeth?	
Can a zebra run?	
Can cows eat grass?	
Can cows fly?	
Do you bounce a ball?	
Do you bounce a glass?	
Do you buy food at the grocery store?	
Do you buy food at the library?	
Do you eat a ball?	
Do you eat cookies?	
Do you get shoes at McDonalds?	
Do you get books at the library?	
Do you get books in the garage?	
Do you get fries at McDonalds?	
Do you like to watch the dirt?	
Do you like to watch videos?	
Does a bus carry people?	
Does a bus say woof woof?	
Does a car drive on the road?	
Does a car swim?	
Does a pillow go in the refrigerator?	
Does a pillow go on your bed?	
Does a sheep say ba ba?	
Does a sheep say moo?	
Does a shoe eat a cookie?	
Does a shoe go on your foot?	
Does a tree grow?	
Does a tree sing?	
Is a cookie dry?	
Is a cookie wet?	
Is a french fry salty?	
Is a french fry sweet?	
Is a spider an insect?	
Is a spider an instrument?	
Is an elephant big?	
Is an elephant small?	

Question

Yes or No	Notes
Is an ice cream cold?	
Is an ice cream hot?	
Will a house drive on the road?	
Will a house have a bathroom?	
Will a lion fly?	
Will a lion run?	
Will a pig fly?	
Will a pig say oink oink?	
Will you eat a box?	
Will you eat cereal?	
Will you sleep in a bed?	
Will you sleep in the pool?	
Will you wear a coat?	
Will you wear a refrigerator?	

Chapter 4

Sentences

There are many forms of sentences that contain different parts of speech. This chapter organizes sentence structures and provides examples that demonstrate the type of sentence that is possible. Blank spaces are left in each category to allow you to make up similar sentences that are functionally relevant for your child. Sentence examples are listed to teach you how to build sentences for your child to learn to say. You should tailor the sentences so that they make sense to your child in his environment. The more practical and relevant a sentence is, the more useful it will be for the child to learn.

These sentence examples demonstrate how you can speak more simply to convey a message. Sentences with fewer parts of speech are easier for a child to understand and to say. For example, the "subject + be + adjective" is an easier sentence to use because it is basically only a descriptor and a noun. Sentences with more parts of speech are more complicated.

The parts of speech for each sentence type are listed in the category name. The sentence examples show you how the parts of speech come together to make a sentence. You should focus more on the form of the sentence and less on the words in each sentence, because these are only examples.

There are a few ways to teach sentences. They can be practiced as imitation where you say the sentence and the child repeats it. You and the child can both read the sentences. Or another option is to write the words of a sentence on individual pieces of paper and have the child put the words together like a puzzle. You can write the sentences on paper and leave out certain words and instead make an underlined blank for the child to fill in another word.

Sentence

I + Verb + Noun	Notes
I am a boy.	
I can read.	
I drink water.	
I eat cookies.	
I go to school.	
I have blue eyes.	
I have brown hair.	
I hear an airplane.	
I like cookies.	
I like to play computer games.	
I live in a house.	
I need a crayon.	
I play the guitar.	
I put Pooh on the table.	
I ride in a car.	
I see the cat.	
I smell a banana.	
I use a toothbrush.	
I want a hot dog.	
I wear shoes.	

Pronoun + Be + Adjective	Notes
He is busy.	
He is noisy.	
He is tall.	
It is broken.	
It is small.	
She is happy.	
She is mad	
She was tired.	
They are quiet.	

Sentence

Sentence Stem	Notes
Can I	
He is	
It is	
She is	
That's a	
The boy is	
The girl is	
The kids are	
The man is	
The people are	
They are	
We are	
You are	

Subject + Adverb + Verb	Notes
I always cry when I'm sad.	
I always fall asleep late.	
I never brush my hair.	
I sometimes skip dessert.	
I usually brush my teeth.	

Sentence

Subject + Be + Adjective	Notes
The apple is red	
The car is red.	
The chair is green.	
The chips are salty.	
The cookie is sweet.	
The elephant is big.	
The giraffe is tall.	
The lion is big.	

Subject + Be + Location	Notes
He is on the bus.	
I am in the kitchen.	
It is on the sink.	
She is over there.	
They are on the train.	
We are in the car.	
You are on the couch.	

Sentence

Subject + Be + Noun	Notes
A banana is a fruit.	
A chair is furniture.	
A giraffe is an animal.	
Cake is a dessert.	

Subject + Be + Verb	Notes
He has to work.	
He is drinking water.	
I am playing the computer.	
I am sitting.	
I am sleeping.	
I am swimming	
She is drinking coffee.	
She is playing with the doll.	
She is watering the plant.	

Sentence

Subject + Preposition + Noun	Notes
He's at the beach.	
It's around the corner.	
It's next to the book.	
She's in the kitchen.	

Subject + Verb	Notes
The baby sleeps.	
The bear ran.	
The boy cried.	
The boy draws.	
The cat eats.	
The dog jumped.	
The girl rides.	
The man drinks.	

118

Sentence

Subject + Verb + Location	Notes
The man is in the boat.	
The woman rides the bus.	
The boy is in the ball pit.	
The dog lies on the bench.	
The dog jumped up.	
The girl is climbing up.	
The girl sits at the table.	

Subject + Verb + Noun	Notes
He blows the candles.	
He plays cards.	
She rides a bike.	
She went down the slide	
The boy colors a picture.	
The boy eats a muffin.	
The dog bites the man.	
The dog jumps the fence.	
The girl reads a book.	
The girls jump rope.	

Verbal Behavior Targets - A Tool to Teach Mands, Tacts and Intraverbals

Sentence

Subject + Verb + Noun + Location	Notes
Mommy feeds the baby in the high chair.	
Rain falls on the flowers outside.	
The boy went down the slide at the park.	
The cat eats the food in the bowl.	
The dog jumps up in the snow.	
The dog sits on the bench.	
The girl brushes teeth in the bathroom.	
The girl cooks food on the campfire.	
The girl floats on a raft in the pool.	
The girl raises her hand at school.	
The girl rides her bike outside.	
The kids play cars on the floor.	
The kids play in the house outside.	
The kids play with the truck in the sand.	
The farmer feeds animals on the farm.	
The man pours water on the campfire.	
The man puts the pizza in the oven.	
The man throws the dough in the air.	
The people roast marshmallows over the fire.	
The woman buys groceries at the store.	

Chapter 5

Category, Feature, and Function

Category

A category is a group of words that have attributes in common. For example, animals, food, and furniture are categories. This chapter provides lists of single and multi-attribute categories. Children will often categorize new words based on their attributes, this grouping may help them learn and recall words. Children can be asked to list items in a category, such as; "Tell me some clothing" or "Names some colors.". Categories can be used to define a word such as "A dog is a pet." or "A chair is furniture." Consult your language program for other uses of categories. Also consider using the targets in chapter 1 that are organized into useful categories.

Feature

A feature is a descriptive attribute of an object. Features offer an opportunity to categorize and group words. For example, list some things that are hot or things that are big. Features allow children to expand on their understanding of an object and how it relates to other objects. A child can learn to describe an object such as "a car has wheels, doors, lights, a horn and a driver". Features help them make comparisons and contrasts with other objects, such as: "a dog and a cat have tails, they are pets, and they have whiskers. However, a dog has floppy ears and a cat has pointy ears."

Function

A function is an action or ability of something. For example, a dog barks, scissors cut, and a light shines. Like features, functions are useful to help put words in context, to group words that are similar, and to use words together in phrases and sentences. A child can use functions to build requests. He can say open door, tie shoes, or pour milk as requests because he has learned that those are functions of those objects and they are meaningful in his environment.

It is effective to teach words in groups of other words, to put words in context, and to consider the category, feature, and function of each word that you teach.

Category

Category	Notes
accessories	
aircraft	
animal parts	
animals	
bathroom things	
beach things	
bedroom things	
birds	
boats	
bodies of water	
body parts	
books	
breakfast foods	
buildings	
candy	
clothes	
cold things	
colors	
community workers	
dinner foods	
dishes	
drinks	
electronics	
exercises	
fairy tale	
family	
farm things	
food	
footwear	
fruit	
furniture	
games	
headwear	
holidays	
hot things	
ingredients	
insects	
instruments	
jewelry	
kitchen	
land forms	

Category	Notes
letters	
lunch foods	
materials	
meat	
money	
nature	
numbers	
outside things	
people	
plants	
playground things	
restaurants	
rooms	
school things	
sea life	
seasons	
shapes	
silverware	
sky things	
snacks	
songs	
space	
sports	
stores	
summer things	
things that grow	
tools	
toys	
vegetables	
vehicles	
water animals	
weather	
winter time	
workers	

Category

Category + 1	Notes	Category + 2	Notes
animals - farm		big farm animal	
animals - forest		crunchy salty food	
animals -insects		hard sweet food	
animals -ocean		small forest animal	
animals - pets		small home animal	
animals – zoo		soft sweet food	
drinks - cold			
drinks - hot			
drinks - sweet			
food - breakfast			
food - cold			
food - dessert			
food - dinner			
food - hot			
food - lunch			
food - salty			
vehicle - 2 wheels			
vehicle - 4 wheels			
vehicle - air			
vehicle - land			

Feature Likeness

Feature	Likeness	Notes
banana / apple	fruit	
bicycle / tricycle	wheels	
car / truck	vehicles	
cereal / eggs	breakfast	
circle / square	shape	
cookie / cake	dessert	
cow / pig	farm animals	
eyes / nose	face	
giraffe / zebra	zoo animals	
guitar / piano	instruments	
hot dog / bacon	meat	
juice / milk	drinks	
Legos / puzzles	toys	
mom / dad	family	
pants / shorts	wear on legs	
pen / pencil	write with	
penny / quarter	money	
pretzel / potato chip	snacks	
refrigerator / stove	kitchen	
window / door	open	

Feature Difference

Feature	Difference	Notes
airplane / train	sky / tracks	
apple / banana	red / yellow	
banana / orange	yellow / orange	
boat / car	water / street	
book / video	read / watch	
car / motorcycle	4 wheels / 2 wheels	
cat / dog	meow / woof	
ears / mouth	listen / talk	
elephant / mouse	big / small	
eyes / nose	see / smell	
hat / shoes	head / feet	
laugh / cry	happy / sad	
plate / cup	food / water	
rock / pillow	hard / soft	
sidewalk / street	people / cars	
sock / pants	foot / leg	
sun / moon	day / night	
tree / flower	big / small	
water / coffee	cold / hot	
winter / summer	cold / hot	

Feature

Big	Little
elephant building bridge airplane train	ant mouse button key coin

Crunchy	Greasy
chips pretzels cereal lettuce carrots	bacon french fries chips pizza lotion

Hard	Soft
ground baseball bat metal road	pillow feather couch bed kitten

Orange	Yellow
orange carrots basketball pepper juice	banana school bus egg yoke sun squash

Has wheels	Has a tail
car bike motorcycle truck shopping cart	dog airplane pig horse cat

Feature

Round	Flat
circle	paper
cookie	mirror
Frisbee	cookie sheet
sun	glass
moon	plate

Hot	Cold
fire	ice
sun	water
stove	snow
grill	air conditioner
candle	ice cream

Sour	Sweet
lemon	cake
lime	ice cream
grapefruit	candy
sour milk	sugar
sour cream	cookies

Sharp	Wet
knife	snow
scissors	rain
paper edge	swimsuit
blade	raincoat
saw	fish

Wood	Plastic
table	toy
bat	plate
chair	cup
handle	fork
log	bag

Function

Blow	Drive
balloon bubble horn trumpet nose	car truck fork lift motorcycle van
Open	**Flies**
jar door box present can window	airplane bird helicopter eagle jet kite
Throw	**Peel**
ball frisbee newspaper trash tantrum hands	banana apple potato onion wrapper
Make	**Carry**
picture bed card list schedule	box backpack luggage paper bag baby
Wash	**Write**
clothes hands dog car face	a story a letter a book a sentence an invitation

Function

Cut	Brush
paper	hair
hair	teeth
fingernails	dog
in line	paint
food	horse

Push	Pour
grocery cart	water
stroller	juice
chair	milk
door	gas
swing	salad dressing

Play	Ride
music	horse
board game	bike
computer	motorcycle
sports	scooter
video game	jet ski

Pop	Wear
bubble	coat
corn	socks
balloon	hat
blister	shirt
soda	ring

Fill	Drink
bucket	milk
cup	soda
mouth	juice
plate	water
box	lemonade
back pack	tea

Chapter 6

Conversation Topics

Conversation topics can be used in numerous ways to support a child at different times during his language development. Each topic provides common phrases that can be used to talk about that topic. Features, functions and categories are written in short phrases. Ideas of possible activities that can be performed with the conversation topics are listed in order of complexity. Teachers should select ideas that suit each individual child's needs.

Language Activities

Beginner

- A teacher can say an easier version of the phrase or just say some of the nouns and verbs in a phrase.
- The student can imitate saying multiple words about a topic.
- The student and teacher can take turns making a comment about the topic using the list of phrases.
- The student can list phrases about the topic.

Intermediate

- The student says a group of features or functions about a topic.
- The teacher will ask questions which the student answers in a phrase.
- The student can read the phrases and make an additional comment.
- The student can expand on the phrase by personalizing the meaning to himself with additional information.

Advanced

- The student makes up a question and the teacher says a phrase as the answer.
- The student reads the phrases and puts them into complete sentences.
- The student says a synonym or an opposite for a word in the phrases.
- The student uses the topic as a story starter and creates a drawing and sentences that use the topic. The student adds fictitious names for story characters and additional descriptive details.

Activity – Daily

Go to Bed	Wake up
take a bath put on pajamas brush teeth go to the bathroom read a book put head on pillow get under the covers close your eyes go to sleep	open eyes stretch arms and legs say "good morning" get out of bed go to the bathroom wash your face get dressed eat breakfast brush your teeth
Go to School	**Eat Dinner**
wait for the bus get on the bus go in to school hang up coat put away backpack read a book write your name say "hi" to teacher say "hi" to friends	use manners set the table get the food eat with a fork cut with knife use napkin eat food drink water clean up dishes
Get Dressed	**Play a Game**
pick out clothes put on underwear put on shirt put on pants put on socks and shoes check weather to pick a coat or not put on a hat	find a friend to play with pick out a game open the box get the pieces set up the game roll the dice play the game
Watch TV	**Do Chores**
turn on TV pick a show to watch watch TV laugh at funny things talk to friends about the show turn off TV	help around the house pick up clothes put away dishes hang up coat throw away trash make your bed

Activity - Fun

Tag	Beach
play with kids chase a kid tag his shoulder say "you're it" run away fast play in the grass play outside have fun	wear swim suit put on sunscreen wear sunglasses use a pail and shovel play in the sand build a sand castle splash in the water sit on the blanket dry off with a towel
Camping	**Picnic**
camp in the forest walk in the woods set up a tent make a fire roast marshmallows zip up sleeping bag see the stars at night	go to a park sit on a blanket drink lemonade eat a sandwich play Frisbee rest in the sun watch for ants
Ride a Bike	**Go to Movies**
put on your helmet wear safe clothes check your tires push the pedals ride safely check for traffic	pick a show buy ticket buy popcorn find a seat be quiet watch the movie
Go to a Ball Game	**Go to the Library**
buy tickets take your glove make a sign find your seat buy peanuts cheer on your team go to the bathroom	find books talk to the librarian use the computer check the shelf use your library card check out books take books home to read

Animal

Horse	Dog
is a farm animal people ride says neigh lives on a farm wears a saddle has a mane has a tail has 4 legs eats hay drinks water wears horse shoes pulls a wagon	barks says woof woof has 4 legs has a tail runs likes to be pet is a pet lives in a house is an animal has paws is taken for a walk wears a leash
Cow	**Cat**
makes milk says moo eats grass lives on a farm is a farm animal is big has 4 legs has an udder has a tail drinks water	purrs says meow has whiskers has 4 paws has a long tail drinks milk eats cat food jumps up is a pet lives in a house
Zebra	**Elephant**
has black stripes has a white body looks like a horse has a tail lives in a zoo eats grass has 4 legs	has big ears is grey has 4 legs has a long trunk has a tail eats hay lives at the zoo
Whale	**Fish**
is an ocean animal is a big mammal eats little fish swims in the ocean splashes water has a spout	eats plants lives in the water swims around can be a pet has gills has fins

Animal

Bird	Bear
lives in a tree	lives in the forest
sleeps in a nest	eats honey
makes a nest from sticks	eats plants or meat
eats worms	sleeps in the winter
flies in the sky	is a big animal
has wings	is black or brown
has a tail	has 4 legs
is a small animal	can walk on 2 legs
lays eggs	is fat
has feathers	has fur
says tweet tweet	hibernates in the winter
Bee	**Spider**
makes honey	is an insect
says buzz	is black
is an insect	has many legs
flys in the sky	crawls in the house
can sting people	lives outside
is small	scares people
help flowers grow	makes a web
live outside	eats insects
is yellow and black	
Frog	**Giraffe**
has two eyes	has a long neck
swims in the water	has spots
can be green or brown	eats grass
likes to jump	lives in Africa
says ribbit	lives at the zoo
lives near a pond	is very tall
has 4 legs	has 4 long legs
Turtle	**Squirrel**
has a hard shell	has a bushy tail
likes the water	has two eyes
walks very slowly	eats acorns
is green or brown	lives in the forest
has a little tail	runs up a tree
has 4 legs	is gray
	has fur

Art

Paint	Scissors
comes in colors makes a picture is put on a brush is wet needs to be covered when done is messy can stain clothing	are sharp open and close have a handle have blades used for cutting handle carefully cuts paper
Glue	**Paper**
is sticky is white squeeze it out put on paper sticks things together	is flat comes in many colors can write on can draw on can cut shapes from
Crayons	**Tape**
used for drawing used on paper comes in many colors made of wax are sharpened hold in your hands store in a box	is clear is sticky used to put stuff together fixes a tear have to rip it put on paper used for wrapping a present
Pencil	**Eraser**
is a writing tool must be sharpened has black lead made of wood writes on paper has an eraser	on the end of a pencil fixes mistake rub on paper makes marks disappear is flaky

Electronic

TV	Telephone
plug into the wall has shows is heavy connects to a DVD player turn it on turn up the volume has a remote	has numbers has buttons rings talk to people say "hello" answer it make a call
Computer	**Clock**
turn it on play games on it has a mouse has a keyboard is a machine has a battery has a screen	has batteries has hands tells time on the wall has numbers plug it in may have an alarm
DVD Player	**Refrigerator**
plays videos connects to the TV plugs into the socket has buttons is an electronic needs electricity has a remote control plays movies	is an appliance keeps food cold in the kitchen is cold has milk and meat has a door plugs into the wall
Shampoo	**Vacuum**
use to wash hair is a cleaning product found in the bathroom used to clean hair mixed with water makes bubbles comes in a bottle squeeze out	has a handle cleans floor has a bag picks up dirt plug into the socket push it use it on the carpet makes a loud noise

Event

Barbeque	Birthday Party
cook on a grill eat hot dogs and burgers serve potato salad eat salad have friends over sit outside use napkins has cold drinks	invite friends sing "Happy Birthday" blow out candles get presents eat birthday cake eat ice cream play games say "Thank you" for presents
Fair	**Movies**
see farm animals play games win prizes ride on rides see exhibits eat ice cream watch shows	drive to the theatre buy tickets get popcorn buy candy find seats be quiet watch the movie
Wedding	**Recess**
people dress up see the bride and groom listen quietly go to the party eat good food dance to the music sit with family see lots of guests	get in line play outside go down the slide chase friends listen for the school bell climb the ladder go on the jungle gym play ball games
Museum	**Parade**
go to the city buy tickets get a map see the exhibits don't touch read about the exhibit listen to a story	go to town find a place to sit sit in the crowd watch the floats listen to the bands see the balloons see banners

Food

Apple	Hot Dog
red or green	is meat
is a fruit	is brown
has skin	eat for lunch
crunches	put on ketchup
eat it	is long
is a snack	eat in a bun

Banana	Cake
is yellow	is a dessert
is a fruit	is sweet
is soft	has icing
has a peel	eat at a birthday party
eat it	can have candles
peel it	get a piece
it is a healthy snack	bake in the oven

Cookies	Cereal
are round	is a food
are sweet	eat it with a spoon
are crunchy	put it in a bowl
bake in the oven	pour on milk
are a dessert	is crunchy
have chocolate chips	eat it for breakfast
are small	comes in a box

Carrots	Bacon
are vegetables	is brown
are orange	is greasy
are crunchy	is meat
grow under ground	fry in a pan
eat in a salad	have for breakfast
are a good snack	is crunchy

Food

Egg	Chips
is a food eat for breakfast fry in a pan is round is white and yellow can have it scrambled	are a snack are food are salty are crunchy can be white come in a bag made from potato or corn
Ice Cream	**Juice**
is a dessert is cold can be chocolate comes in a cone eat it lick it is made from milk taste sweet	is a drink made from fruit pour it in a cup can be orange can be apple have with breakfast drink it have it cold
Milk	**Orange**
is a drink comes from cows is white is cold kept in the refrigerator pour on cereal drink from a glass	is a fruit grows on a tree has a peel is juicy is round you peel it you eat it
French Fries	**Peas**
are a food made from potatoes are white are greasy taste salty eat with your fingers get at McDonalds	are small are green are a vegetable eat them have for dinner are round taste sweet

Food

Bread	Pretzels
make sandwiches is sliced has a crust is white can be toasted is chewy have for lunch	are salty have a twisted shape are brown eat as a snack are crunchy come in a bag
Hamburger	**Candy**
is round is meat put on a bun put ketchup on it get at a restaurant is greasy is brown	is sweet is for dessert comes in many colors can be hard is delicious can be chewy eat just a little
Turkey	**Potato**
meat has legs has breast has wings fill with stuffing eat at Thanksgiving put on gravy has brown meat has white meat	is white is a vegetable cook in the microwave boil in water mash put on butter shake on salt can bake in the oven can peel off the skin
Sandwich	**Salad**
made with bread put on mustard put on mayonnaise has turkey or ham has peanut butter and jelly eat at lunch time put on a plate	has lettuce has tomatoes put on salad dressing put in a bowl is crunchy has cucumber eat for lunch or dinner

Holiday

Easter	Valentine's Day
hunt for eggs boil eggs dye and paint eggs see the Easter bunny get a chocolate bunny get an Easter basket see Easter lily eat jelly beans	make red hearts give presents say "I love you" give cards say "Be my valentine" eat chocolate have a party
Christmas	**Halloween**
is on December 25th Santa Claus comes we give presents we get presents we decorate the Christmas tree we eat a big dinner we go to church Christmas is in the winter	is on October 31st I wear a costume a witch flies on a broom I see ghosts we carve pumpkins I say "trick or treat" I knock on doors I get candy
Thanksgiving	**Fourth of July**
you eat turkey have a big dinner visit with relatives give thanks for family have pumpkin pie eat cranberry sauce have mashed potatoes clean up all the dishes	go to a parade see fireworks carry the American flag wear red, white and blue go to a carnival have a picnic eat hot dogs celebrate America
Labor Day	**New Year's Day**
last day of summer vacation is first Monday in September is before school starts celebrate people who work there are sales at the stores many people don't work	sleep in is the first day of the year no school watch football have friends over have snack foods

Verbal Behavior Targets - A Tool to Teach Mands, Tacts and Intraverbals

144

Household

Bed	Bathtub
is furniture you sleep in it has sheets has a pillow has blankets found in the bedroom	fill with water is in the bathroom get inside take a bath put in bubbles pull the drain

Chair	Cup
is furniture has legs has a seat has arms you sit on it goes with a table	gets filled up in the kitchen gets empty you drink from put in juice put in water washed in the sink

Dish	House
is flat put food on it can be plastic may be ceramic might break put dinner on carry to the table put in the dishwasher wash after a meal	has doors has windows has a roof is where people live has rooms has a garage is in a neighborhood has a yard

Knife	Shampoo
is a piece of silverware use it to cut food it is sharp we are careful with it keep it in the drawer has a handle goes with a fork	is a cleaning product found in the bathroom used to wash hair mixed with water makes bubbles comes in a bottle squeeze out

Household

Book	Flashlight
has pages has words has pictures read it it tells a story open it close it turn the pages	turns on turns off makes light use in the dark has a switch uses batteries helps you see at night use when camping
Fingers	**Elevator**
have 5 on each hand one is a thumb have nails have knuckles use to touch things wear rings can bend can make a fist	goes up goes down has buttons stops on floors has a door carries people has a bell is in a building
Piano	**Key**
is an instrument makes music is black has white and black keys gets played has a bench is in an orchestra is big	opens locks use in a door made of metal keep on a key chain use to drive a car carry in your pocket
Door	**Table**
made of wood may have a window has a handle open it close it knock on it in the house	made of wood made of glass put dinner on put chairs under use in the kitchen use in the dining room have one outside

146

Outside

Flower	Grass
grows outside has a stem has petals smells nice looks pretty is a plant needs water grows in the dirt put in a vase	is green is in the backyard gets mowed has weeds is long and thin need to water it
Moon	**Rain**
is in the sky can see at night is bright is big shines light changes shapes is in space	falls from the sky made from the clouds gets you wet falls on the ground makes puddles is a type of weather
Ocean	**Snow**
is full of water has fish has whales is salty has a beach has waves can swim in it	Is white Is cold is a type of weather falls in the winter used to make a snowman people ski on it people slide on it
Sun	**Tree**
is hot is yellow shines in the sky is in space makes the daytime is bright gives you a sunburn is a star	grows outside has leaves has branches has a trunk in the forest needs water some bear nuts some have fruit

Place

Playground	McDonalds
go down the slide climb up the ladder run around go up and down on see saw climb the monkey bars play in the sand play with kids go on the swing	has golden arches has a playland play with the kids jump in the ball pit buy a happy meal eat a burger get french fries go to the bathroom
Library	**Grocery Store**
search on the shelf look at books borrow books get CDs be quiet listen to a story take books off the shelf check out materials	push a shopping cart use a list look at vegetables get potato chips buy meat pick out apples put fruit in a bag buy the food
Zoo	**Farm**
many animals live at a zoo animals live in cages people walk on the path go to the gift shop don't feed the animals monkeys make noises zoo keepers feed the animals	barn is red cows eat hay chickens lay eggs horses run in the field sheep are behind the fence rabbits are in a cage vegetables grow
Space	**Restaurant**
space has planets earth is a planet we live on earth astronauts fly in space astronauts wear white suits astronauts fly space shuttle space shuttle blasts off	sit on a chair read the menu give order to waiter use good manners eat food drink water go to the bathroom

Place

Mall	Store
ride the elevator go up the escalator walk around go to the Disney store get a snack go shopping sit on the bench	look for toys or clothes play with toys put on clothes buy the toys pay with money or credit card get a bag say "Thank You"
Gas Station	**Post Office**
drive to the gas pump pick up the gas pump put in the gas pay for the gas get a snack inside wash the car windows	park in the parking lot go into the post office wait in line talk to the postal clerk buy stamps mail letters send off package
Airport	**School**
where airplanes land where airplanes take off check your baggage where you get on an airplane fly in the airplane eat food at the airport pick up people ride the escalator	has classrooms kids learn at school has teachers go to lunch have recess go to the library read books write stories

Season

Summer	Fall
wear shorts go to the park wear sunscreen wear sunglasses go swimming see leaves on the trees play in the sprinkler	it gets cooler the leaves turn color the leaves fall it gets windy we have Halloween we rake leaves wear a coat
Winter	**Spring**
it is cold it snows wear a coat and hat wear boots and mittens make a snowman play in the snow	it rains the flowers bloom the grass grows the birds tweet use an umbrella wear a rain coat

Sport

Baseball	Soccer
swing a bat throw a ball run the bases catch the ball play on a team wear a baseball cap	throw a soccer ball kick a soccer ball play on a team make a goal run down the field
Basketball	**Tennis**
shoot a basketball make a basket aim for the hoop run down the court play on a team wear shorts and sneakers	swing the tennis racket run after the ball hit the ball play on the tennis court play with another person wear tennis shoes
Football	**Golf**
play on a football field has teams played by football players uses a brown ball ball gets kicked players fall down	play on a big course use golf clubs hit a little white ball hit the ball into a hole walk on the grass ride in a cart
Swimming	**Hockey**
go to the pool wear a swimsuit use a floaty throw a ball jump in the water wear goggles take a shower dry off with a towel	played with a stick shoot a puck get a goal wear a helmet wear padding wear gloves wear skates play on ice
Ski	**Volleyball**
wear skis wear boots go on the snow do in the winter go to the ski resort go down the hill fast ride up in a chair lift	hit a ball go over the net play on a team use a white volleyball try to score use your hands don't let it hit the ground

Worker

Police officer	Farmer
wears a uniform wears a hat carries a gun helps people drives a police car fights crime gives speeding tickets	works on a farm grows food weeds the garden drives a tractor feeds the chickens weeds the garden milks the cows
Fire fighter	**Waiter**
wears a fire proof suit drives a fire truck uses a fire hose sprays water puts out fires climbs a ladder	gives you a menu takes your order brings you to your seat gives you food pours your water works in a restaurant
Doctor	**Dentist**
helps sick people works in the hospital gives you medicine checks your temperature wears a white coat looks in your mouth looks in your ears weighs you talks to mom and dad	wears a mask cleans your teeth gives you a new tooth brush works in an office has a big chair uses dental floss talks to mom and dad wears gloves uses bright lights
Pilot	**Teacher**
flies an airplane wears a uniform has a hat sits in the cockpit uses the controls talks to people on the airplane lands the airplane	works at the school teaches children gives you lessons reads you books likes children teaches how to read

Worker

Lifeguard	Chef
wears a bathing suit saves swimmers works at a pool swims in the water says "no running" watches the people keeps people safe	works in the kitchen makes people food mixes food uses the stove puts pans in the oven wears an apron chops vegetables
Cashier	**Mail Carrier**
works at a store uses the cash register helps you buy things may wear an apron takes your money puts things in a bag gives you change	wears a uniform carries mail and packages fills up a mail box drives a jeep walks in the neighborhood delivers the mail asks people to sign for packages
Delivery Person	**Bus Driver**
delivers packages to people wears a uniform drives a big truck uses a dolly to carry big boxes asks people to sign their name carries boxes goes to a warehouse to get boxes	drives a bus takes children to school takes adults to the city asks people to be quiet keeps riders safe on the bus drives carefully parks the bus at the garage
Librarian	**Janitor**
works in a library helps you find books reads a story uses the computer puts books on the shelf gives you a library card sit in a chair stand behind the counter	wears a uniform empties the trash cleans the floor works at the school works in buildings fixes things in the building cleans up a mess wears gloves

Vehicle

Airplane	Car
pilot flies carries people places takes off from the airport flies in the sky lands on the ground has a tail has wings is a big vehicle has loud engines	has 4 wheels has a trunk has doors has windows has an engine carries people drives on the street parks in a parking lot goes in the garage
Bike	**Motorcycle**
has 2 wheels has handle bars you ride it it is fun has a chain has pedals riders wear a helmet	has 2 wheels has an engine is noisy drives on the street carries 1 or 2 people requires a helmet goes fast
Fire Truck	**Ambulance**
is a vehicle has ladders has a siren has a driver has wheels goes fast carries firefighters has hoses parks at a fire station	is a vehicle has a siren has a driver has wheels goes fast carries sick people goes to the hospital has medicine has emergency workers
Train	**Boat**
goes on a train track has an engine carries people and things has a caboose has an engineer is long has many cars	floats in the water carries people may have a sail may have a motor gets wet goes in the ocean used for fishing

Verbal Behavior Targets - A Tool to Teach Mands, Tacts and Intraverbals

Data Sheet   3 columns

1			
2			
3			
4			
5			
6			
7			
8			
9			
10			
11			
12			
13			
14			
15			
16			
17			
18			
19			
20			
21			
22			
23			
24			
25			
26			
27			
28			
29			
30			
31			
32			
33			
34			
35			
36			
37			
38			
39			
40			

Data Sheet   4 columns

1				
2				
3				
4				
5				
6				
7				
8				
9				
10				
11				
12				
13				
14				
15				
16				
17				
18				
19				
20				
21				
22				
23				
24				
25				
26				
27				
28				
29				
30				
31				
32				
33				
34				
35				
36				
37				
38				
39				
40				

Data Sheet

2 sets

1				
2				
3				
4				
5				
6				
7				
8				
9				
10				
11				
12				
13				
14				
15				
16				
17				
18				
19				
20				
21				
22				
23				
24				
25				
26				
27				
28				
29				
30				
31				
32				
33				
34				
35				
36				
37				
38				
39				
40				

Data Sheet   5 columns

1					
2					
3					
4					
5					
6					
7					
8					
9					
10					
11					
12					
13					
14					
15					
16					
17					
18					
19					
20					
21					
22					
23					
24					
25					
26					
27					
28					
29					
30					
31					
32					
33					
34					
35					
36					
37					
38					
39					
40					

Index

Introduction 1

Chapter 1 – Words 2

Noun

Noun (continued)

Chapter 5 – Category, Features, and Functions

Chapter 6 – Conversation Topics

References

Skinner, B.F. (1957). *Verbal Behavior.* Englewood Cliffs, NY: Prentice Hall, Inc.